14 DAYS TO ALASKA

Two Brothers in a 57-Year-Old Airplane Fly the
Ultimate Cross Country Flight Training Adventure

Troy Hamon

ISBN 978-1-59433-257-9
eBook ISBN 978-1-59433-290-6
Library of Congress Catalog Card Number: 2012933243

Photos by Quinn Hamon
Cover drawing by Rebecca Hamon
Maps by Rebecca Hamon
Cover by Swanky Designs, LLC

Manufactured in the United States of America.

DEDICATION

In which I most sincerely thank my wife, Rebecca, for living with me even though I am both a pilot and an airplane owner. Either one of these afflictions is more than any normal person should be expected to bear. Both of these together must be hard to endure. And yet she has done it, and continues to do it, with grace and humor. Thank you, Becky.

FALLING FROM THE SKY

In which I introduce the story at its
most dramatic moment

As we reached 800 feet above the surface of the earth over Heath, Ohio, the engine quit. Luckily we were flying at 80 mph at the time, and the air hitting the propeller caused it to windmill in front of the airplane as the nose pitched down and my brother, the flight instructor and expert pilot, took control.

"My airplane."

"Your airplane."

This had seemed like such a good idea. I wanted to learn to fly, and I wanted an airplane. I had bought the airplane and he was helping me learn to fly in it, then we were going to bring it back to Alaska together. But now, that plan was changing in moments, reduced to a simple mission of how to land without destroying both ourselves and the admittedly meager investment I had made in this ancient airframe.

I was assigned to change the fuel selector, in case the problem was related to the fuel tank we were operating on, while Quinn made sure we kept the airplane in the air as long as possible while he started looking for a place to make a safe emergency landing.

Below us were wooded areas and some congested streets. No good landing option was immediately apparent...

PRESSING AHEAD INTO SUBOPTIMAL CONDITIONS

In which I relate another of the pivotal moments of the adventure, when weather and time conspired against us, or at least made us sweat a bit

As we flew up the valley toward Haines Junction, the clouds got lower and lower. After having been stuck in Whitehorse by low ceilings and ice fog, we were running out of days. At the very least, we hoped to get Quinn to Anchorage so he could make his flight. It had crossed my mind a few times that this might involve leaving the airplane somewhere highly inconvenient. Like Canada. But we had what had appeared to be a window of opportunity to get into Alaska based on the weather reports along the route, so we had taken off and headed toward Northway. Now, however, we were dropping down, flying along at 1,000 feet above the ground, peering through the haze ahead at distances that looked deceptively small, but in reality might have been as much as five miles. But to my unaccustomed eye it looked like really poor visibility. And regardless of what the numbers were, I had been watching it get poorer and poorer.

Thinking about the clouds and visibility made me tense. And every time I got tense, I went up…which made the problem worse. As I climbed, I could see less, and Quinn would lean on the yoke over on the co-pilot side and tell me, yet again, to hold my altitude.

"Okay…"

"When you climb up it makes it worse, not better."

"Right, but I'm not climbing because I want to."

"Well, don't."

As we passed Haines Junction, Quinn illustrated the actual visibility to me, which was indeed well over three miles, but then as we turned north and followed the highway toward Silver City, the visibility continued to deteriorate. I was looking at the map, making sure we had room to turn around if need be. And Quinn was doing the same thing…

But perhaps we'd best start at the beginning, or even a little before…

PROLOGUE

In which I try to rationalize the craziness that causes a 38 year old male, successful but not wealthy, to decide to learn to fly an airplane

Major life changes come in all shapes and sizes. Some people buy fancy cars, others abandon their families, and many change occupations or move to a new location. It's usually a good idea to limit the number of major life changes that you encounter at any one juncture. For example, when you are expecting your first child, it isn't the best time to move, or to start a new job. Being a logical, rational person, when my wife Becky was expecting our first child and we were living in Seattle, I applied for a job in King Salmon, Alaska.

To complicate matters, I was hired, and we moved during the ninth month. That was complicated. So much for listening to the conventional wisdom. King Salmon was an adjustment for us, but we stuck it out and grew to enjoy it. Almost from the first winter we were there, some of our family members asked whether we were going to buy an airplane. Actually…the thought had never crossed our minds.

It had apparently crossed my brother Quinn's mind though. After getting a degree in electrical engineering and looking around for jobs, he realized that the job he wanted wasn't an engineering job. It was a flying job. So he went back to school, this time flight school, and worked his way through the various levels of flight training, then started moving into jobs of increasing seniority until now he is living in Columbus, Ohio, and is the chief pilot for a freight company that flies Lear Jets.

Through the years, I occasionally considered learning to fly, but my interest was more on being dropped off in the wilderness than on turning around and flying home. This meshed well with my work as a scientist for some of the most spectacular national parklands in the country, situated in remote Alaska.

But as the years passed, I began to be less and less satisfied to desert my children in order to spend time in the wilderness. And as I moved into more senior jobs, much of the fieldwork was being done by other people anyway. And where we live, pilots usually sleep at home. And, and, and. Hmm…let's see…

Although I enjoy my work, and yes I still love fieldwork, I also enjoy the straightforward logistical side of the operation. As one of the boat operators for the park, I am occasionally responsible, as the boat operator, for getting people from one place to another. And I really enjoy doing that. I could get people and gear from one place to another for a living if I was a pilot, and I'd probably enjoy it. Hmmm….

There are no airplanes for rent in King Salmon. In fact, every person I know here who has learned to fly has done it by purchasing an airplane to learn in. In the summer of 2007, I made a comment to Becky that I was interested in buying an airplane and learning to fly. This is the part of the story where her job is to tell me that it isn't practical and we need to wait or save money or do something more logical.

But her response? "That would be fun…"

Excuse me? Like many conversations where we throw our thoughts out in order to have them kicked around and exposed for the foolishness they are, I was expecting to have this one quickly deconstructed into utter nonsense. Her response shocked me. After some discussion, it turned out that she also thought it might be good for me to look at other career opportunities. So there we were, apparently sharing a mid-life crisis in which we both thought I might be better off preparing for another occupation. But there were contributing factors…

King Salmon can only be reached by air. There are no roads connecting King Salmon to anything more than 15 miles away, so while we have vehicles for local use, we can't actually go anywhere. No weekend road trips, or for that matter, road trips of any sort. In theory, with a really large boat (for safety) and an unearthly amount of fuel, you could get somewhere by sea. But to get to Anchorage (and any trip anywhere starts by getting to Anchorage, when you live where we do…) you would have to travel over 1,000 miles on the water. And that trip would take you to some of the most dangerous marine waters on earth.

The Bering Sea, down which we would need to travel to get to the end of the Alaska Peninsula, is the site of the infamous crab fisheries made even more famous by their depiction on "Deadliest Catch," and is noteworthy for the danger of the deadly combination of cold water and horrible storms. False Pass, where we would pass from the Bering Sea to the Pacific Ocean, is one of the windiest places on earth (although, all of southwest Alaska probably qualifies for that distinction). On the other side of the peninsula, we would have to travel up Shelikof Strait, renowned for the number of vessels beneath the water. And then, we'd have to travel up Cook Inlet, which even Captain Cook himself hated, with its thirty-three feet of tidal action.

No thanks.

So finally, we arrive at the initial option… to get anywhere you have to fly. Of course, there are commercial flight services that fly us around out here. But as our family has grown from three to four, and the children have both long since passed that magic 24-month age where they must have their own seat on the airplane, the cost of purchasing seats has become a bit prohibitive.

Bush flights in Alaska are expensive. I don't know whether they should be or not, but they certainly are. It often costs more for us to fly the round trip from King Salmon to Anchorage, which is less than 300 miles each way, than it does to fly round trip from Anchorage to most locations within the contiguous 48 states. Yes, you read that correctly. Our little 300 mile leg costs more than some of the multi-thousand mile legs between more major airports.

So one of the gradual effects of the costs of air travel on our little family has been that we don't travel often. We try to make the trips long enough to make a difference when we do go, but it doesn't happen often by any stretch. So my wife, it turns out, was partly just interested in something that allowed her to travel more… not more overall, just more often, even if the trips were shorter. Me learning to fly might help. Us owning an airplane and me learning to fly would certainly help.

I was so shocked and excited by the possibility of buying an airplane that I talked to practically every person who crossed my path about it. Many of them responded by asking the primary question. "You're buying an airplane? So are you a pilot then?"

Well, no, not yet…

Most local people in King Salmon understand the situation, though. The people that I know who learned to fly here did so after buying an airplane. But at some point when I was sharing this wild new thought with Quinn, the professional pilot brother, he had something else to offer…buy it down south and he would help me fly it to Alaska.

Now, that sounded cool indeed. In fact, he had spent years in the training department at the company he worked for, had maintained his flight instructor credentials, and would be willing to instruct on the way. That sounded more than cool! And it meant I could look at planes in any region of the country, really.

GROUND SCHOOL

In which I study and enjoy it, and infect
another soul with airplane mania

I tend to be a bit obsessive. At least, if you believe my wife. Perhaps it would be more accurate to say that when I get interested in something I study it incessantly until I either get a grasp on the information or run out of new information to process or actually wear myself out. So I consulted a local flight instructor about what I needed to buy, and bought it. A textbook, flight computer, plotter, and assorted other stuff. And just to be thorough, I bought another textbook. I read the textbooks, both of them, all the way through… and thought maybe I was ready to take the test.

But you can't take the test in King Salmon, and I didn't get around to taking it over the winter. So I went ahead and took another look at the textbooks… except I couldn't. The second time through was just too repetitive even for me.

So I bought a DVD course and watched that. Along the way I'd infected another poor soul, Paul, with flight mania, and he had an old VHS course. It turns out he had done most of the training for a private license but marriage and family caught up with him and he never finished. He was interested in learning to fly and sharing the cost of the plane. Actually, he works as an airframe and powerplant mechanic (A&P), so his contribution in terms of labor was more than equivalent to my contribution in terms of dollars.

Anyway, we watched his video course as well. Which turned out to be a bit painful... the teaching style didn't really mesh with our personalities. But we got lots of dubious entertainment mocking the instructors!

After repeated studying, taking practice tests on my computer, and trying to brush up in areas that weren't as familiar to me, Quinn sent me a logbook endorsement, because I had, on average, been scoring well over 80%. The minimum passing score for the FAA written exam is 70%, so I was reasonably certain I would pass.

When Quinn sent the logbook endorsement, he included a message. "Since my name is now associated with this test, I expect a minimum of 90%!" Okay... back to the books.

After some more practice tests, I arranged to stop in at Take Flight Alaska at Merrill Field on my way through Anchorage. My practice tests were usually about 40-50 minutes. I told my wife to come back in about an hour and I'd be ready. Luckily she knew better than to listen, and took the kids off for a longer sojourn.

First of all, there was some preparatory work involved in verifying that I was ready for the exam, preparing the exam computer, briefing me, the test-taker, on the test process, and generally settling in. Second, there was the fact that in my practice tests, I tended to hurry through and just see how I did. There would be no hurrying this time. I read every answer to every question. So when all was said and done, I took a bit longer.

But it was worth it. The lady preparing my exam results report smiled, "You did very well." Oh? Good! Turns out I missed 3 questions. So my final score was 95%, which I immediately called and told Quinn about. He seemed to be satisfied, albeit somewhat grudgingly. "That'll do... I guess..."

AIRPLANE SHOPPING

In which Paul and I end up settling on an
airplane that isn't really what either of us want

I had started airplane shopping in the fall, but all the airplanes I wanted cost too much. Often way too much. Airplanes I might be able to afford tended to be either so small that there was no potential use for them beyond training, or they were in such sorry shape that they weren't airworthy. And many of the aircraft in question used a lot of fuel.

Becky was interested in a four-place airplane. Two-place aircraft use less fuel, a lot less in some cases. My initial interest was in a Maule, which is a great little Alaska plane with four seats. I'd flown in one once, and sat in the back seat. All 6'4" of me. If I could fit back there, it must be okay for a family. Paul was a little less excited about a Maule. Turns out he isn't real fond of working on tube and fabric aircraft.

Aircraft come in a few different fundamental constructions. Many modern aircraft are being designed and built from composite materials, which allows sleek modern forms. Before the advent of the composite designs, most aircraft were being constructed from sheet metal designs in which the body of the aircraft is formed from sheets of metal that are much of the structural integrity of the aircraft. But before sheet metal aircraft, there was another phase...

Actually, tube and fabric isn't just from back in ancient history. There are still tube and fabric aircraft being made new, such as the Maule I still dream of. The basic structure is just like it sounds. The airplane is constructed from steel tubes that are welded into an airplane-shaped cage. Fabric is stretched over the cage, then tightened down by heat and chemicals and painted to form a strong exterior surface.

From an economy point of view, tube and fabric tend to be lighter weight, which reduces the engine size, which reduces fuel burn. At least in theory. I had downloaded a database of single-engine aircraft performance numbers and combed through it obsessively, and that was one of the conclusions I came to. However, Paul was definitely more in favor of metal, so I started looking at early version 172s.

I found a few that were perhaps affordable, though the lower end of the price bracket started to look like aircraft that would need lots of work. But they all flew Continental engines. Paul had primarily worked on Lycoming engines, and was more comfortable with that, so I went back to the drawing board.

I found an aircraft that was affordable, powered by Lycoming engines, with four seats. But it was a fabric aircraft. They were generally very affordable though, so we found ourselves looking at Piper PA-22 aircraft, commonly known as Tri-Pacers, or, somewhat mockingly, flying milkstools. Seems not everybody thinks they're attractive. Not a particularly great airplane from a performance standpoint, but with careful planning we could haul our family of four a couple hundred miles safely. Until the kids put on weight, that is. Hard to stop that, though...

Still, it seemed worth starting out on the margin of too small given that the first year would see mostly just me or Paul and an instructor or me or Paul alone in the plane.

Buying old airplanes is a bit of a challenge. The primary problem being they're... old. But we waited around and finally found one that had critical parts (fabric, engine) in good shape for a reasonable price and bought it. N624A. A very cute little white and red number that looked a little bit like a 50's diner inside. My wife suggested we wear bobby socks and sip cherry Cokes while we flew. This was May. That's when I requested time to make a training/ferry flight, and was given October.

October!? It's busy in Alaska in summer, so that's pretty much the best we could do.

We had a while to wait, so Quinn went to Texas and picked up the plane, then flew it to Columbus, Ohio, where he lived. In fact, our parents went to visit

Quinn with N624A at KVTA. He flew it to Ohio from Texas.

Quinn and Dad with N624A at KVTA. Dad flew a PA-22-108 (also known as a Colt, a similar plane but with only two seats) as a student pilot in the 1950s. Quinn is demonstrating that he (and I, we're the same height) is not taller than the airplane. Barely. Dad would probably fit a little better than we did...

Mom with N624A at KVTA. My mother got to see the airplane before I did. She said it was, "cute." Great. I think.

and he took them out to see the plane as well. Since it was originally in Texas, near the home of one of my three brothers, that brother saw it as well. So I had one brother that didn't see it before me...but other than that I was the last one to see it from my family.

After passing the written exam in June, I was immediately thinking about the next step. Since, given my summer schedule, my boss authorized the trip in October, I had a long time to wait and forget stuff. In my typical fashion, I thought maybe I'd get some texts on instrument flying, the next big challenge after getting a private pilot certificate. But it seemed like a lot to try to digest when I hadn't even learned to fly yet, so I never did talk myself into it.

In the end, I mostly just waited out the summer. I had subscribed to AOPA Flight Training magazine, which helped remind me of things I had learned (and was letting slip away due to inactivity…). And whenever I could lay my hands on an old copy of a flight magazine I would read it through from cover to cover. Twice. Or three times. Sometimes I even understood some of it…

WELCOME TO FLIGHT TRAINING

In which I make my first takeoff and successfully fly around without any disasters before my brother lands the airplane while pretending to let me do part of it

By the time October came, I had been chomping at the bit all summer. Every good weather day I imagined flying... but couldn't. Whenever I flew in a small plane for work, I peppered the pilot with questions. My excitement was tempered by the knowledge that with an aircraft as old as ours (57 years at the time of purchase...) there were going to be a lot of little maintenance issues that would add up to something big over time.

We had some inspections done that had brought up some issues we needed to address at the first annual. But the airplane had really not seen significant amounts of use in its entire life, so we expected to find some issues it had during our ferry flight, as the long legs and extended flight hours would push it beyond the levels of use it had seen in the previous ten years.

I left home on my anniversary (oops... not ideal planning that...) and arrived in Columbus on my birthday (on the other hand, it certainly was a worthy birthday present, so hard to fault that...) to be met at the airport by my brother.

The next day we went out to Newark-Heath airport, KVTA as it is known in the shorthand used by the aviation world, to see the plane, look it over, and start flying. Sort of odd…why not Columbus? They have airports there, don't they?

Of course there are airports in Columbus. Quinn was looking for an airport that was relatively simple for my introductory experience. This seemed odd to me. I would have to learn to fly in airports with control towers to get a license anyway (and like everything else about flying, even my limited initial understanding was almost universally off-kilter… there are no pilot licenses… instead I would be getting a pilot certificate… but I hadn't recognized that minor distinction initially…). But the airports in Columbus are not just tower-controlled, they are busy, tightly regulated with massive numbers of aircraft coming in and out. We'd have to spend a lot of time waiting for air traffic control to get us in and out of the airspace, not to mention taxi to and from runways when we were on the ground, and he felt it might be a bit overwhelming to start that way the first few flights.

So he had hunted around and identified KVTA as a nice little airport where we had plenty of runway (over 4,000 feet) without too much air traffic to deal with. Newark and Heath are smaller towns that sit a few miles east of Columbus in deciduous woodlands, and were still nicely green in early October.

There were quite a few ladies that were excited for me to be training at Newark. And no, it had nothing to do with aviation… the Longaberger Basket building, which is shaped like a huge woven basket, is there. Even in King Salmon, Alaska, people know about Longaberger baskets. At least, my wife's friends do.

The building must be described, at best, as a bit of an oddball. Though I mean that in the best possible way… It is not on the shortest path to the airport, though, so I never did see it from the ground. I imagine it would make a fairly impressive structure from ground level. Newark is also somewhat well-known among other circles of which I must confess I am not a part, for the large earthen mounds left by the Hopewell Culture. I don't know how impressive those might be, because I wasn't sufficiently tuned in to even look for them…

In contrast, nobody seems to have much interest in Heath. As far as I can tell, the only noteworthy thing about Heath is an Air Force Base that has no aircraft. Oddly enough it is situated right off the end of the airport, but I never noticed it when we drove by it every time we headed to KVTA, including that first trip. The population of Heath is much smaller than that of Newark, but KVTA is actually in or adjacent to Heath, while Newark is a couple miles away.

We did an extensive preflight that first day, talked about the order and nature of preflight inspections, and spoke with the maintenance shop about the aircraft. One of the funny things about preflight inspections is that I remember that first one as extensive. But I inspect more things now on preflight inspection than I did then, so really it was less extensive. But when you are new to the aircraft, and new to flying, the sheer detail of a preflight inspection is a bit staggering. And since Quinn had to explain the purpose of every part of it to me, and I had to figure out what he was talking about as I peered intently at each moving part, it took a long time.

The following day we got up and went to the airport to start flight lessons. Which started with my second preflight inspection, just as thorough but not nearly as long, then we were actually in the airplane and getting it fired up.

Wow.

I had, one time previously, handled the controls of a small private airplane during taxi, which had seemed very foreign as I'd never in my life steered with my feet before. I still wasn't having an easy time of it on this second attempt, either. I kept grabbing for the steering wheel, which is actually a control yoke and not really a steering wheel.

"Take your hand off the yoke, you don't handle an airplane with that on the ground.

"Take your hand off the yoke."

And again, the next time my hand strayed up there… "Take your hand off the yoke."

Quinn was typically understated, repeatedly asking me why we weren't taxiing on the yellow line anytime we strayed more than a few inches off it. "Just wondering if we were turning off into the grass… or making room for a phantom airplane… or perhaps going over to see if we could ding the prop on installations along the edges of the taxiway or runway…"

The first takeoff didn't seem as difficult as I expected, but then I started learning about all the things I wasn't doing right.

"Put your hand on the throttle.

"Put your hand on the throttle.

"Keep your hand on the throttle and don't take it off.

"Put your hand on the throttle. Yes, it's all the way in, but if it slips you need to be able to put it back in full without delay. Next time start putting some back pressure on when we reach rotation speed, you waited too long. After the airplane is in the air, you need to keep it over the runway all the way to the end of the runway, then maintain the direction straight off the runway until you either turn crosswind or exit the pattern. Make sure to maintain the airspeed that gives you the best angle of climb until you are at pattern altitude. Then, if you are going to continue to climb you can either maintain the same climb attitude, or use a cruise climb attitude."

Whew.

Okay.

On the same previous day that a (foolish?) pilot had let me steer an airplane on the ground, I had done some little bit of handling of the aircraft in the air. The experience had shown me that maintaining altitude is not easy, and that turning is not so simple either. But it had given me a bit of experience trying those things. On this first training flight with my brother, we went up to 3,500 feet out in a relatively calm area of airspace and did a couple of shallow bank turns. Then a couple medium bank turns. "And don't forget those clearing turns! You need to make a couple of 90-degree turns while actively scanning the airspace because you want to make sure there are no aircraft in the area before you start any of these maneuvers!"

I apparently did okay on the shallow and medium bank turns, because Quinn then said it was time to try steep bank turns. He described what I was going to do. There is no artificial horizon in N624A, so I'd need to maintain a steady visual reference to the horizon using the support bars in the windshield.

So I rolled the airplane into a 45-degree bank and around we went. Except that it didn't really work out as Quinn had wanted. In fact, from a pilot performance standpoint, my steep bank turns were a miserable failure. I couldn't maintain airspeed, or bank angle, or anything properly. Frankly, they were scary. About when I found myself getting pushed down in my seat by momentum, I'd start to feel like I was doing something wrong. Except I wasn't, that was how it should feel, so everything I did after that was messing it up, as I tried to alleviate that pressure rather than fly with it. But you have to put a bunch of additional force on the seat of your pants to perform a steep turn properly.

Oops.

A couple not so satisfactory attempts, then my brother showed me how it should be done. Hmm... it really does sit you down in your seat. And, at least to me, at least the first time, it was more than a bit scary. He allowed as how that isn't usually a first flight maneuver, but I was doing well so he thought we'd give it a try.

Okay, well that made me feel a little better...

Finally, back to KVTA for my first landing.

Well, I didn't do so well in the pattern...

"Entering downwind, slow to 80 mph, here's the checklist, may as well prepare for future training so use the full GUMPS list (Gas from desired tank, Undercarriage for retractable gear that doesn't apply to N624A but you don't ever want to forget that as part of your checklist when you do fly retractable gear aircraft, Mixture full rich or set appropriately for high altitude landing, Prop setting for constant speed prop that doesn't apply to N624A but again you want to be ready to include it when you are flying an airplane with a constant speed propeller, and Safety, which in our case is primarily seatbelts fastened).

"Slow down to 80.

"Slow down to 80.

"This airplane glides like a brick so your pattern will be closer to the runway than other aircraft, you need to get used to establishing it at the same point off your wing strut so you can fly it the same every time.

"That looks good.

"Slow down.

"When we get abeam the numbers at the end of the runway where we're going to land you need to reduce power to 1500 rpm and maintain airspeed. This aircraft has two levels of flaps so we will put in one notch on base leg and the second on final. When the runway end is approximately at a 45 degree angle behind the wing, turn to base.

"Slow down.

"Don't forget to announce your actions.

"Watch your airspeed.

"Slow down. Put in one notch of flaps. Turn final.

"Slow down. Announce final. Line up with centerline of the runway."

Of course, in reality we were weaving all over the place, every radio transmission was wrong, I couldn't seem to maintain airspeed at 80, it just felt scary flying that slow, and I basically had no idea what I was doing. I felt the occasional control nudge coming from the copilot controls as Quinn kept me out of trouble.

"Keep your hand on the throttle. Apply power. Now!" I felt his hand on mine, applying the power he had asked of me. The controls began to work on their own accord, as he made the landing I was trying to screw up, and then relinquished control to me for braking with the funky bar brake.

We taxied off the runway. "Announce clear of the runway. Why are we not on the yellow line? Slow down. Park over there."

Whew!

A sort of hilarious hopelessness when you looked at my overall performance, but I was undaunted: "When can we fly again?" Sort of an odd mix of feelings afterward. I didn't feel very competent up there, but by golly I'm going to learn...if I don't scare off my instructor? He claimed he wasn't scared.

That's good, because I was, especially that landing business. Didn't make any sense to me when to do what or how much. Confusing. More practice needed...and more to come. And where was that Longaberger building, anyway? Must have missed it...

WAITING...AND MORE FLIGHTS

In which the schedule is destroyed, the importance of being able to land the airplane is made mightily apparent, and yet I am still unable to do so

The morning following our first mind-bending flight, my brother had competing commitments and we couldn't fly. I wasn't too worried. After all, we had a whole seven days to work with. We had agreed that if we could get 7-10 days of flying in before we took off, I might be able to get my private license at the end of the trip. That would mean enough time to solo prior to departure, then a layover somewhere where I could do a solo cross-country. Or that could happen at the very end.

Anyway, with the thought that I needed somewhere around 20 hours to solo, it seemed like it could work. But we really only had mornings, as my brother was working from noon to late at night each day. And here we were missing one day. Still, not a catastrophe. I took the opportunity to watch (again...) the video course I'd purchased, and paid special to the section on steep turns, stalls, and landings—watched those sections over and over, so I'd be mentally prepared.

The next morning...thunderstorms, low clouds, rain... no flying that day.
The next morning...beautiful blue sky! Until we got near KVTA...fog,

fog, fog. Went to McDonald's to have a coffee and talk about things. Among other things, I was reminded that during landing, when he asks for power it needs to be applied quickly and it needs to be a substantial power increase. We finally got back to the airport as the fog lifted ... but we were out of time.

Okay, need to recalibrate. Not looking like the pre-departure solo is going to happen. I wasn't really in a big hurry, as my only flight so far was overwhelming to the point that I felt no great hurry to be left alone in the cockpit. Before leaving for work, Quinn pulled his original log book out of his safe and told me to enjoy looking it over. "You're probably going to be feverishly looking at how many hours before I soloed."

Actually, by the time he said that I was already poring through it, but I was busy looking a bit further on, seeing the extensive listings of training flights he conducted for other students and what they did. I had to confess to him that I was in no great all-fired hurry to solo, given that I knew I couldn't handle the aircraft yet and was still a bit scared at the thought of being in it by myself.

Of course, after his comment, I did go back and look at his first few pages of the logbook. His time to solo was 37 hours. Wow. And he had 137 landings before solo. Wow. It looks like maybe I'll be getting to that later, based on missing some of our relatively limited window for pre-trip training. But the next day we did get to fly, and since Quinn doesn't work on Fridays we managed to make two training flights.

It was a beautiful day, and taking off was pretty interesting this time. I was trying to figure out how to stay over the runway. The airplane wanted to turn left ... just like they always said in the training materials. High power setting, low airspeed, apply right rudder to maintain coordinated flight.

Amazing! It works, and it feels a lot better!

Quinn pointed out that it also helps greatly to have an aiming point on the horizon that is in line with the runway since the runway itself will disappear beneath the airplane during takeoff. It certainly felt like a major improvement. And the plane was not quite so foreign or scary, either. We headed north to our practice area, did two clearing turns, and tried a couple steep turns. It was fun! I had convinced myself that they would be, was mentally prepared for the increased seat pressure, and flew two steep turns to the practical test standards (PTS) of the FAA, as Quinn informed me afterward.

Next up: stalls! Quinn showed me an approach to landing stall and recovery, then had me do it myself. I was excited to do them, as all the time watching the instructional video had mentally prepared me for viewing it as a fun and positive side of training. But the reason they are part of training is that they can also be deadly if pilots aren't vigilant.

An airplane flies by moving the wing through the air fast enough to generate lift. The wing is roughly straight on the underside and curved over the top. As the air moves over the curved upper surface, it must move faster than the air passing under the wing. The faster movement of the air over the top of the wing results in a lower pressure above the wing in comparison to below, which leads to lift.

This action of lift is changed by the angle that the wing encounters the air. As the front of the wing tilts up (the angle of attack become higher), the air moving over the top of the wing starts to break free of the wing surface and move in a turbulent fashion at the rear of the wing. As the angle of attack increases, there comes a point where the turbulent flow advances forward far enough that the wing is no longer capable of producing sufficient lift to keep the airplane flying. This is a stall. Stalls can be easily recovered so long as the aircraft is not spinning and there is sufficient altitude. In takeoff or landing phases, there is often not sufficient altitude, so recognizing the feeling of a stall that is about to begin is even more essential.

In my hands, the stall developed quite a bit more than when Quinn was flying. I was not trying to make a rapid recovery, which in retrospect seems odd, but I was really interested in feeling a stall and hadn't thought far enough ahead to focus on recovery with minimum altitude loss. The departure stall was similarly benign when Quinn flew it, but more developed in my hands. Clearly some additional practice needed, but stalls were not scary after all. Of course, if they occurred near the ground, that might be a bit different…

After another forgettable landing attempt, which Quinn saved for me (again), we took a break and went to have some lunch. He reiterated the importance of being ready to add power during the approach to landing. Now… it seems like it might be important; he says it like he means it in the air, he reminds me repeatedly on the ground… hmm…

Afterward, we returned to KVTA for a pattern flight, my first.

We were standing next to the airplane when Quinn asked, "Are you in a hurry to get in and get going?"

"Well, I don't have any other plans… why do you ask?"

"I'd like to see this Lear land downwind."

So I looked up and sure enough, there is an airplane turning final for runway 27. Runway numbers are the first two numbers of a three-digit magnetic bearing. So due magnetic west is 27, due magnetic east is 09. Of course, magnetic degrees are always off, but runways are numbered based on compass bearings so pilots don't have to run mental math while preparing to land to convert from the compass in front of them to the runway heading.

So there we were, and in came a jet. With a tailwind. The runway is 4,629 feet long. All of these details were sort of lost on me at the time. What did I know? The jet landed and got stopped at … 4,200 feet or so. Quinn was just shaking his head. Hmm …

He then looked up and spotted more aircraft coming in. Three more, in rapid succession. All three were small low-wing aircraft. They were also coming in for downwind landings on runway 27, so we stood and watched them approach. Two of the three took up 4,000 feet to land, the other taxied off at midfield, so by extension used only a couple thousand feet. Again, Quinn was shaking his head.

"So, why are they landing downwind like that?" I wondered, fairly innocently, since I couldn't conceive of a downwind landing at that point, or for that matter, any landing in which I did it myself.

"Well, as far as the Lear crew, they saved three minutes of fuel by choosing a downwind landing on a short runway with no margin for error. Having given themselves no room for error, they made no error and everything worked out. The small planes should all have been able to land with ample room left over even with the tailwind, so less of a safety factor, but two of them were unable to make the landings short enough to maintain that safety margin. Amazing."

He shook his head as we got in the aircraft and prepared for flight. Takeoffs were making sense to me now. Too bad that was the easy part. The entire traffic pattern seems simple enough, but each phase has its own challenges. After takeoff, flying straight out from the runway, is the upwind phase. Then, in the standard traffic pattern you make a left turn and fly crosswind perpendicular to the runway. This is followed by another left turn to downwind, which brings you back parallel to the runway, then a left turn to base, another left turn to final, and the landing itself. In some locations where the traffic pattern consists of right turns, it is referred to as right traffic.

"Keep lined up over the runway well out past the end of the actual runway. Turn crosswind and announce, continue climbing. Turn downwind and announce. Level off, begin arrival checklist (Gas, Mixture, Safety) and prepare (mentally) for descent. Abeam the numbers, pull power to 1500 rpm, maintain straight flight path, turn base and announce. One notch of flaps, continue descent, turn final and announce. Second notch of flaps."

Whoa! Plane ballooning … gaining altitude all of a sudden after pulling the second notch of flaps) … all sorts of adjustments needed …

Quinn was getting lots of practice helping me figure out landings, "Add power, lots of it, ease back off … (we land) … flaps up, power full on, repeat. This time let's leave off the second notch of flaps. It doesn't do much to reduce stall speed in this plane, so let's work on getting the landing picture in your head before we add that."

Speaking of my head, I was trying to get my head back in the game. Crosswind, downwind, checklist, descent, base, final, a little better, still can't feel this emergent need for power changes that Quinn urges me to make. Do it again, and again, and again, then full stop and park it for the day.

Whew.

A couple of those were a little better, but it just seemed like I was missing some major sixth sense that Quinn had in spades. He claimed this was normal... which should be reassuring since the normal pilot seems to have managed to learn how to land. And once again I failed to look for or see the Longaberger building. How can one go to Newark and not see the Longaberger building?

There were quite a few aircraft piling up in the parking area, some of which had landed while we were flying the pattern. Quinn went to see what was going on the following day, Saturday, to see whether we were going to be limited by some massive increase in weekend flight activity.

He came back, chuckling. He couldn't wait to bug the lady that he says is one of the best pilots in his company. It seems that all the downwind landings were people arriving for a Women in Aviation conference. Speaking of which, when I thought about it, women were pretty scarce in my flying experience. Maybe my daughter will want to learn to fly... or even my wife...

Another night to watch the videos obsessively. Which, of course, I did.

HEART STOPPAGE

In which we arrive at the scene with
which I began this tale of adventure

The next day, we were back for another pair of training flights. The first was a repeat of the morning flight from the prior day, in which we explored steep turns and stalls. This time, I did great on the turning portion, but didn't pay attention to headings going into or out of the turns.

Whoops.

Both directions I was more than 10 degrees late emerging from the turn. For the flight test to get a pilot certificate, I will need to roll out of the turn on the same heading that I was on when I rolled into the turn, a perfect 360 degree circle. I was doing more than a full circle. But it was fun! Still, I guess it would pay to keep practical test standards in mind when I'm trying to do maneuvers. And it just makes sense.

You don't likely find yourself in flight needing to do a turn for the simple sake of it being fun … it is because you are turning to a heading. So better keep that in mind for the next round.

Stalls again… and again no improvement over previous flight. Still letting the stall develop too much, over-correcting, losing a lot more altitude than necessary.

And then, for something a little different, practice with emergency approach to landing. This was a surprisingly benign exercise. Power is reduced to idle while you're flying, and as the engine stops pulling you through the air (okay, it's actually the propeller that pulls you through the air, but that's only because it's hooked to a running engine…), the airplane pitches forward and you start descending. But, and this is important…you are still flying. The first thing to do is to trim to best glide speed, which is the speed at which you'll be able to travel the furthest before reaching the ground. According to the Short-Wing Piper Club, that is 90 mph for this airplane. I got it to 90 and then started looking around. I was thinking of fields, but my brother was thinking of roads. The little skinny roads between the fields. The ones that tend to have power lines strung along beside them. I realized that the primary difference was confidence. He actually could land this little plane on any narrow little dirt road that presented itself, let alone something large enough to be paved. Me? I was thinking about huge open spaces… obviously I need to learn to land this thing.

We experimented with a couple of other glide speeds, but the recommendation of 90 seemed pretty spot-on. Same descent rate as 80, but with more distance covered, which might be the additional distance needed. Back to the airport, "shouldn't we be able to see the Longaberger building?"

"Oh, yeah, it's over there somewhere."

And sure enough, it was. Very unimpressive from miles away, but it was visible. So I actually did see it, but maybe we'd get a closer look later… ?

Meanwhile, we were approaching the airport for another attempt at landing… which was, well, let's just say… still not setting any records. Good thing there's an instructor in the plane.

We took a break, where I got a bunch of feedback. "You seem to like working hard, you never trim the airplane for the phases of pattern."

"You mean you would trim for each pattern leg?"

"Well, yeah, but I'm a lazy pilot, I don't like to work hard. It's lots more work to fly without trim."

Aircraft can have multiple trim systems, but our Tri-Pacer has only one. It controls the angle of the horizontal stabilizer. The horizontal stabilizer is what most non-pilots might think of as the "back wings." They aren't actually wings, in that they don't provide any lift… in fact in level flight they are angled so there is a downward force applied on them. On most aircraft, the center of gravity (CG) in the airplane is in front of the wings. This means that if you suspended the aircraft from a single cable, the location where that cable attached to the airplane would need to be at some point in front of the wing (or at least, in front of the spot on the wing where lift is at its greatest) in order for the airplane to hang straight without tilting. The engine is a big chunk of metal out in front, which usually is responsible for the weight distribution necessary to create that frontal CG.

If that were the whole arrangement, the weight of the engine would cause the plane to nose over and point down. This is a good thing when the engine stops, which we had experienced in a measure with the emergency practice that morning. But the rest of the time it would merely prevent flight rather than assist it. The horizontal stabilizer acts by creating a downward pushing force on the tail of the aircraft when air is flowing. The amount of force exerted is affected by the aircraft speed and the angle of the stabilizer. Pulling or pushing on the control yoke moves the rear portion of the stabilizer up and down and allows the pilot to change the pitch quickly with direct control. But for stabilized flight, it is better to angle the stabilizer so you don't have to push or pull constantly, and that's what the trim system does.

In the Tri-Pacer, this is accomplished by turning a large jack screw that is attached to the front of the horizontal stabilizer. Turning a little crank up above the cockpit turns a cable that goes back and turns the jack screw, lifting or dropping the horizontal stabilizer.

Another thing to think about in the pattern!?!? And I'm already overloaded! And I don't get this landing thing!

We also went through detailed weight and balance calculations, had a soda, and headed back to KVTA for another pattern flight. And it got…interesting. We had done all our routine checklists, taxied out to the runway, waited while idling for some other traffic that was using the airport, then taxied out onto the runway and took off.

The aircraft is not a stellar climber under the best of conditions. That little 135 horsepower Lycoming hanging off the front was a game little unit, but the plane has stubby little wings and there were two very large gentlemen sitting in the front seat. We were climbing up through about 500 feet and I was looking at the airspeed indicator, and the vertical speed indicator, and we were climbing at 80 mph, as per usual. But it didn't feel right. Something was a bit anemic about it, even taking into account the fact that it was a bit of an anemic climber to start with. I was trying to form words to ask Quinn whether he noticed something wrong. But I never got the words out.

Around 800 feet up, the airplane abruptly lost power.

…Wow…!?!?!

My little simulated engine out emergency earlier in the day was very unimpressive in comparison. And the worst part of the situation was that I knew

I couldn't land the plane. Every landing had been done only through the assistance and input of Quinn.

Thank goodness he was in the plane!

And what an eye-opening view of your instructor! He was all business. The instant the plane lost power, the nose pitched down, making it easy to establish best glide. But he instantly took over; "My airplane."

"Your airplane."

He took the controls, established glide, and started looking for a place to land, as well as pulling on carb heat and ordering me to switch fuel tanks.

In a Tri-Pacer, the fuel tank selector is along the wall next to the pilot's leg. There was no way he, in the co-pilot seat, could access it, so I had to take care of that for him.

"Change the fuel." I fumbled around beneath and next to my left leg, switching tanks and making sure the selector clicked into the right spot.

A moment later, the same order: "Change the fuel."

"I did, but here, I'll check it again." Again, I fumbled to make sure it was in the right setting, but it was.

He looked over at me, and repeated again, "Change the fuel."

"I did!" I was looking at him, trying to imagine a way to explain that I had changed it, and ensured that it was properly set up in the detent by feel and appropriately aligned by vision. It seemed there was really no adequate way to express all that in the circumstances, or in the limited amount of time all this was happening in, so he had to settle for, "I did!" After all, the fuel was as changed as it was going to get.

I had been pretty sure I wanted to get it right, so I had rocked it in the detent multiple times, and was pretty sure I wasn't going to do more than exacerbate the situation by fiddling more.

I looked up after spending this time making sure the fuel was properly dealt with, and we were perfectly lined up to land on some road in Heath, OH. Actually, not just any road, but Licking View Drive, a lovely little road that winds along near the wooded hills where we turned from upwind to crosswind on during our previous takeoffs.

I had never driven on Licking View Drive, and hadn't been particularly hoping to. In fact, I'd never heard of it, but I was about to travel on it in what many would consider an inappropriate vehicle. Actually, even I think of it as an inappropriate vehicle. But the mere fact of being lined up on it was especially impressive, because when the power went down, my visual scan suggested nothing. Trees, roads too cluttered by buildings, power lines, intersections, and traffic to be useful…basically nothing obvious.

Quinn admitted later that he had the same first impression, but while I fiddled with the fuel he had persisted in looking for a solution. There we were, all lined up and descending through 500 feet or less, preparing to land on Licking View Drive... and the engine roared back to life!!!

...Wow again...

Talk about music to my ears. No offense to Heath, OH, and certainly none intended to Licking View Drive, but I really wasn't interested in exploring on the ground right then... I suspect Quinn felt the same, because he had seemed really serious when he told me to change the fuel.

Really serious.

We established climb again, and got back into the pattern, coming around for our landing, but went ahead and made it to a full stop instead of the touch and goes we were originally planning on. We taxied off the runway and went straight to the fueling area and asked to have the aircraft fueled.

I watched to verify how much fuel was in each tank, and there was lots. As in more than 11 gallons each side in 18 gallon tanks.

So I checked for water in all the fuel sumps, and there was no water in the fuel that I could find anywhere.

We ran over everything again and again, and concluded that it had to be carburetor ice, commonly just referred to as carb ice. Nothing else made any sense.

The fuel/air mixture in a carburetor is drawn through a narrow spot as it is sucked into the engine fuel lines. The narrowness of the passage at this point reduces the pressure at that location, which draws the mixture in. Both the decrease in pressure and the resulting vaporization of the fuel cause cooling. If the air has water in it, the water can freeze and start to build up on the walls at this already narrow point. Enough ice buildup and all of a sudden there is no way to get the fuel/air mixture to the engine.

Which, as you might guess, can be a problem.

The solution to carburetor icing is to send heated air from around the engine exhaust into the tube to melt the ice. This is typically a problem that is manifested between 20 and 70 degrees, according to the textbooks I had read.

But it was 80 degrees out! Quinn's years of flight training from both sides of the desk had provided the same basic information... carb icing was supposedly unlikely when temperatures rise above 70 degrees. But we couldn't see any other thing that it could be. Consultation with an A&P confirmed the diagnosis.

Quinn looked at me consideringly, then said that he wanted to give my heart a rest so we'd call it for the day.

...But I wasn't having any of that... "Oh, no we don't!"

I told him right then that I didn't want to sit on the ground after that little episode. So unless he deemed the airplane unsafe, I wanted back in the air immediately. I still remember falling off a horse when I was a kid. Actually, since I wasn't the best rider in the family, it happened to me three or four times. Every time, the adult in charge would make me get right back on, even when I didn't want to. At this point in life, I probably have to be the adult in charge … and I don't want to harbor some fear of flying that is made more real by getting scared off for the day. If there was a problem with the airplane, that would obviously be different. But there didn't appear to be any problem …

Okay … so we headed back up.

We did another four or five patterns, in which I made absolutely no progress in using trim during the pattern or in feeling the landing coming like I should. However, I did start to apply power in more appropriate amounts when instructed, so I guess in a sense the control was improving even though I didn't have that sixth sense for sink rate yet. I certainly didn't feel like I was getting any closer. In fact, I mostly kept waiting for the plane to quit.

Which, I'm glad to report, it didn't.

On the final landing, we found we had almost no brakes, and what little we had was completely one-sided. So we grounded the airplane until we could get the brakes worked on, which was Monday.

What a day.

Other than obvious additional attention to my pre-landing safety checklist, which had new emphasis on the act of pulling on carburetor heat (the magic ice-melting solution), most of our conversations over the next couple days revolved around ways to prevent carb icing. I found it interesting that when I looked up carb icing conditions, the particular combination of temperature and humidity was variously depicted in different locations as moderate to severe probability. Might need to update the textbooks I had read, 80 degrees can be bad for carburetor ice. That is, of course, based on my limited experience, but I'm hoping to keep my experience even more limited in the future …

And in order to keep this limited experience, carb heat would become a more pronounced part of my pre-takeoff checklist.

At this point, we had used up our initially scheduled pre-trip training time, and I had only 6 hours of flight to show for it. It looked like the trip was going to be made without a realistic chance of finishing the pilot certificate.

We could stay a few more days, after all it was really only 7 or so flying days to Alaska. Of course, that assumed that the weather was good the whole way. We'd been obsessively checking weather for the whole route for the past seven days, and there were a number of weather fronts moving in and out of the various portions of our planned trip during that time.

It really is not reasonable to plan a trip of this length without provision for weather delays when you're traveling in a small plane. It's not reasonable to plan any small plane trip without provision for weather delays. If we got there with any extra time, we could do additional training at the other end of the trip.

Changes.

Delays.

Inevitable with flight, so may as well get used to it.

FIRST DAY
TOWARD ALASKA

In which we battle endless horizons, numerous

hawks, crowded airspace, and light turbulence

("You call this turbulence?" "Shut up.")

Monday morning, I called the business at the airport that manages the fuel sales, hangar rentals, tie-down rentals (for people that are too cheap to pay for a hangar space... like me...) and aircraft maintenance on the field. The shorthand for a business such as this is FBO, which stands for Fixed Base Operator. Every segment has their own language, and much of aviation's language seems to revolve around acronyms... anyway, the FBO at KVTA is Aviation Works, and I called them to find out whether the airplane was going to have the brakes looked at that day.

The shop called back shortly and reported that 624A would need new brake pads, which weren't available since the brakes were a very old style and the pads would have to be shipped in. If we overnighted them, we might get to leave the next day, but more likely Wednesday. All of a sudden, the three week window for this project was shrinking rapidly. One week gone, another disappearing before my eyes. I asked them to please overnight the pads so we could

39

Ready to depart KVTA. The author loaded up and ready to go. Actually, the copilot/instructor/photographer was loaded up and ready to go as well, but then recalled that he needed a picture before starting this journey.

get the airplane back in service, and spent the day packing, finding things I could mail instead of carry, and generally getting ready.

That evening, I noticed my cell phone had a message on it. Turned out the plane actually hadn't needed pads, it just had a seal on the right brake that needed replaced. This had been done and the airplane was ready by noon. The noon that already had passed. So that was good news, but we couldn't get out the door in time to make any real progress that day anyway. There was a major front that had been sitting over the Rocky Mountains and was trending east slowly, so we hoped to get out to the front edge and sit down underneath it so we could take off into the other side of clear weather after it had passed. Sounded so easy.

Tuesday morning, I went to the airport, preflighted the airplane, loaded it, had it fueled, and paid up my bill at the local FBO for storage, maintenance, and fuel. Quinn went and mailed the boxes I had packed up to reduce the load in the plane, then came back and met me at KVTA. Finally, after months of planning, we took off and established a heading that would take us on the first leg of our journey.

The thought of leaving this little airport behind had me feeling a bit sad. After a grand total of five flights, it felt somehow disloyal to leave the friendly crew from the little business on the field, Aviation Works, and head off into the mysterious distance. On the other hand, it was completely exciting to be starting on this rather epic journey, and working on learning the art of cross-country flight. It is normal for pilots to learn all the details of maneuvering aircraft before launching cross-country, but then I'd never been normal anyway…

The night before, we had laid out the sectionals for the entire portion of the trip across the plains, and put our flight line onto the map in blue highlighter. That line went directly through busy airspace around Columbus, so we headed slightly north of it to a nearby VHF Omni-directional Radio Range, commonly referred to as a VOR (they look like cartoon sombreros sitting out on the landscape), and established a heading parallel to our intended route. The Federal Aviation Administration (FAA) maintains a network of VORs throughout the country, though the Global Positioning System (GPS) has overtaken them for common usage. I was intending to learn to fly the old way before I launched into GPS navigation in flight.

We established a flight altitude of 4,500 feet since that is a flight altitude that the FAA has deemed as acceptable for westerly traffic (180-359 degrees, even thousands five hundred...seems so long ago since I took the FAA written...dredging it back up out of memory...) that is flying with visual reference to the ground rather than by instruments (VFR, or visual flight rules, instead of IFR, or instrument flight rules).

I immediately started getting reminders that I was not doing well with maintaining altitude. Quinn would stare at the altimeter, look at me with mock concern, put his finger on the altimeter, and then ask me if it was broken. Actually, what was broken was my ability to fly level. It seemed like it should be such a simple thing, but I couldn't seem to keep us at the intended flight altitude. We hadn't really gone too far when we started seeing little wisps of cloud ahead, and apparently up at our altitude.

Pretty soon we decided to descend to 3,500, which eventually became 3,000, in order to remain clear of clouds. So long as you are less than 3,500 feet above the ground, the FAA designated cruise altitudes do not apply. Of course, the downside is you might have aircraft coming at you from any direction down there. After getting (mostly) stabilized at 3,000 feet, I again struggled to maintain altitude, busting up and down through my altitude window consistently.

Meanwhile, Quinn was handling charts and establishing navigation procedures for the trip in between bugging me about drifting from my heading and busting my altitude. Unfortunately, these two chores kept him pretty busy, but he still managed to find time for navigation. I'm normally relatively good with direction and orientation. I love maps, enjoy studying them obsessively before I go somewhere new, and look over them at home anytime there is a plausible reason. My wife often rolls her eyes. "There you go, now Troy brings out the maps again..." Guilty as charged.

But flying around KVTA during those first five flights was a bit disorienting because we were focused on maneuvers. I didn't even look at a map during our few training flights (though I did become sufficiently geographically aware to find the Longaberger building...). And now, we were flying over this large, somewhat featureless landscape.

I was appreciative of lakes. They helped a lot as tangible locators on the map. And VORs were really helpful. I'd read about pilots from the early age of aviation getting lost flying cross-country and having to land to ask where they were. Well, I now understand how that could happen. It can be pretty flat out there. But we plowed along, weaving back and forth, up and down, toward Joliet, Illinois, which was our intended destination for the first leg of the flight. We had dialed in the VOR behind us and maintained a heading of 300 degrees away from it. Then we started dialing in VORs ahead of us and using them to establish and maintain our heading.

But Quinn was looking at the airspeed indicator, looking at the progress we were making on the map, and shaking his head. He pulled out my handheld GPS. It isn't an aviation unit, but we had it along in case we found it useful. He decided that it could be useful right then for determining our ground speed. As I got further into training, I'd be doing that without a GPS for help, but he was handling the navigation duties and was feeling lazy. After he got it working, he really started shaking his head. The plane trims out and flies around 120 mph at gross weight, but our ground speed was closer to 85 mph. So we were flying into 35 mph of wind.

We are both 6'4" tall. As the pilot, the rearmost seat location is fine (well okay, perhaps the right word is adequate), putting me just far enough back to have good control movements on the rudders. As an equally tall co-pilot trying not to get in the way of the controls, I'm not sure how he did it. He looked a bit folded up over there.

Apparently, the romance of the trip was waning a bit in the reality of being crammed into the cockpit of this little bug-smasher with an incompetent trainee. I asked him whether that was true, but he said no, he just couldn't bear the thought of flying too long in one day. And since it didn't look like our speed was sufficient to reach Joliet without refueling, he started looking for alternates we could stop at for fuel.

Along our course of flight there were a number of airports, but we selected Porter County Airport, KVPZ, near Valparaiso, IN. In the early stages of the flight, he was sitting over there refolding the map whenever we passed out of one of the map folds. Then, he announced an important moment: we had left Ohio and were over Indiana. After flying over quite a bit of Indiana, on approach to KVPZ we got the weather, and it was a relatively strong north wind (though my definition of relatively strong was anything over a breeze at that point in my training...and I don't recall what exactly it was...but it was blowing from the north...).

"So, we're going to enter the pattern crossing the upwind end of the runway, then entering downwind for runway 36?"

KVTA to KVPZ. Welcome to the Midwest. Did we ever mention that it's flat?
Midwest topography presents itself out the copilot's window early on the first day of flying from KVTA.

KVTA to KVPZ. We're going 120! Take no note of the fact that the airspeed indicator is in miles per hour rather than knots (which is the aviation standard...and faster than mph for the same number...), just be impressed. How often do you get to legally drive your car that fast? Like...never...
Of course, when you consider the 35mph headwind, it gets less impressive...so don't consider that...

"Correct, remember to establish pattern altitude before we enter the pattern, that's 1,770 feet."

I concentrated on following through on that, but losing altitude was not going real well. I was struggling to get the airplane down. It's amazing how hard it can be to make an airplane come out of the air when you have in the back of your mind the fear that the airplane will…come out of the air… You really do have to pull out on the power or increase the airspeed. Again, I wasn't trimming the airplane as effectively as I could have. And I wasn't getting out ahead of the airplane in general. I needed to tell it what to do and make it happen…instead I was thinking about what I wanted to happen, but being too polite to follow through and make it happen.

"Excuse me, Mr. N624A, could you perhaps, if you find it convenient, descend a little bit, say perhaps a thousand feet or so? Pretty please? No? Oh, well that's okay, we'll figure out something…"

WRONG approach to flying an airplane. You don't have to be rude, but it needs to be a more direct interaction.

"Okay N624A old buddy, we're done with flying up here, we're going down. Thanks." I hadn't really figured that out at that stage, however.

There was a lot of activity of other aircraft. I had not yet reached the point where I could make sense of where and how I fit into the pattern of multiple operations. Somehow, despite my failings, I got us down to pattern altitude, into the pattern, and that was the end of where I did anything right.

"Too fast, too close, too little descent rate," were among the things Quinn had to say about that one after I failed abysmally to improve on my previous attempts to land the plane.

Sigh…

We pulled up to have the plane fueled, grabbed lunch and discussed the landing. I probably about drove him crazy. Every landing, I wanted to go over in detail, over and over. Exactly what did I need to change to make that landing work? Exactly where did I mess it up?

The answers were pretty familiar. They started with lateness. I established altitude late, I started descent late, I slowed down late. Late, late, late.

Okay. Going to aim for early next time.

We never ventured further than across the road from the FBO where the airplane was parked, so our experience of Valparaiso, IN was pretty limited, extending only to the truck stop with a Subway in it where we grabbed lunch.

"I don't suppose you can handle the thought of eating while you fly yet, can you?" Quinn asked.

"How could I do that? I'm pretty much overwhelmed just handling the airplane!"

KVPZ to KALO
Chicago in the distance. We were near Valparaiso, and the area had gently rolling terrain with woods and farms in all directions.

"All right, I guess we'll eat here."

Valparaiso boasts a similar number of inhabitants as Newark, OH, but the airport is much larger with two beautiful crossing runways, one of which is 7,000 feet long. Well, 7,001 feet actually. To be precise. Of course, we had landed on the smaller one, which was almost the same as the one at KVTA, so no excuses there. Oh well.

I noticed on a map that there is a Graceland Cemetery not far from the airport.

I wonder if Elvis has been sighted there?

After our dash across the road to grab sandwiches from a truck stop, we were back in the air for the next leg. We were headed for Wyoming, hoping to spend the following night with some friends . For now, we were just hoping to get as close as we could with available time and weather. Based on the rate we were moving, we were going to have to aim for a little shorter than our initial expectations. We took off and started the weave: up and down, side to side.

Quinn would shake his head and tap on the gauges, then I would try to settle into a heading and altitude. I was starting to spend a lot of time trying to make the trim work for me. It helped, but I still needed to pay attention to the altitude and heading. And we were in a bit of turbulence (Quinn seemed to think that it barely deserved the name, but I, on the other hand, was very impressed by it …), which made it harder. The airplane would suddenly bank, or ascend, or descend. I found it rather disturbing for most of that day.

To make it worse, we were approaching the southern end of Chicago airspace. Scary.

As soon as I spent a couple minutes practicing my visual scan, I'd look back and see that I had busted my altitude or heading. Usually my altitude. Correct altitude. Correct heading. Scan.

KVPZ to KALO Passing abeam Chicago. The radio traffic was astoundingly busy. Every time Chicago approach control vectored a plane our way, I would feel like ducking even though they were thousands of feet above us. But I was still having a lot of trouble just hearing what people said on the radio.

How can anyone scan a horizon that's endless? My goodness, it's beyond comprehension! Early in the first leg, I'd asked Quinn about what radio frequency to scan to help with this formidable task.

"Can't we go to the frequency that all pilots use to provide position updates between airports?"

"There is no frequency like that."

"What!?"

"You are responsible for maintaining a scan and making every effort to see and avoid other traffic."

"That's crazy! I'm pretty sure everyone in our area monitors a common traffic frequency and reports their activity and location."

"Well, they may, but there is no frequency established for that purpose other than in the vicinity of an airport."

That seemed totally insane to me, but on reflection it is a bit difficult to see how it could work. Out our way, people use the common traffic advisory frequency (CTAF) to alert people to their actions. But when there are tons of aircraft and airports, how do you divide up the airspace with additional frequencies? Instead of fretting over it, we identified the frequencies of the airports we were passing over, and monitored them.

Now, however, we were on the Chicago approach frequency to keep tabs on anything headed in and out of the major traffic zone there. And the traffic around Chicago was relatively busy. I saw a number of airplanes, all in plenty of time, but not as far away as I'd like. None of them were at our altitude, so in a sense it was never really an issue. But it is very disconcerting to have large engine-driven birds popping up on your visual scan.

I told Quinn that the activity level seemed a bit nuts compared to what I was accustomed to as a passenger in Alaska, and he acknowledged that if he were to buy a personal plane for use in the East and Midwest, it would have to be IFR capable, as it is just easier.

Wow.

Most people I know don't talk about IFR as easier, but then I guess most of the pilots in King Salmon aren't flying Learjets for a living, either. Instrument flight is basically flight without visual reference outside the airplane, so it usually means going through a cloud layer. That's a more advanced level of flying that was beyond the capability of our airplane, and certainly beyond any low-time student pilot.

As we moved on past Chicago, the turbulence increased in frequency. That didn't help my altitude practice. It also came with a steady helping of birds. Real, as in feathered, birds. Hawks actually. Lots of them.

Every thermal in the Midwest must have a hawk riding it. And they all seem to concentrate between 2,000 and 3,000 feet, which was our altitude range for much of the flight. Since they are so small, it was always pretty late before I would see them. They never ended up being in our flight path, but it still seemed to make me jump. Very nerve wracking as a novice know-nothing pilot to share airspace at all, let alone with all these creatures that just appear out of thin air (or so it seemed) a few hundred feet away. Every time I saw a hawk, or two, or three, I would gain a couple hundred feet. Oops.

Before we knew it, we were flying over the Mississippi River north

KVPZ to KALO I'm either going so fast or weaving up and down to dodge hawks, so I'm blurry. Hopefully that will prevent my wife from noticing the 80s-man shades I'm wearing. They're not her favorites.

KVPZ to KALO The Mississippi River is visible in the distance as a ribbon of light near Savannah, IL, as the adventurous duo finds themselves heading under a layer of clouds ahead. We were trying to make headway before a storm arrived, hoping to sit down under it overnight while it passed overhead. Sometimes plans like those work. This time, in fact, it worked.

KVPZ to KALO
Somebody needs to shave. And don't let my wife see me in those sunglasses...she hates them...

of Savannah, IL. What an impressive sight it was! Huge; a massive break in the regularity of the groomed fields with islands and sand bars and navigation buoys and boats, as well as heavy vegetation along the edges. We oohed and ahhed over it for a while, since we got to fly along it briefly before it turned north away from our flight path.

Then we started looking at how far we were going to make it before the next fuel stop. We had been speaking about Hampton, IA, but weren't sure about pushing it that far since we were still flying into a pretty good headwind. We settled on KALO, Waterloo Regional Airport north of Cedar Falls Iowa.

Along about this time, my brother acknowledged that he had fallen down on the job and failed to announce our passage into Iowa. He then excused himself, because it occurred simultaneous with the crossing of the Mississippi River, and wasn't marked at the location where our blue high-lighter line crossed the river. Subsequent lapses of similar nature eroded this justification, however...

We chuckled a bit about the happenstance that we had overflown Illinois without even stopping. And right in the middle of one of the most memorable presidential campaigns in history, too! Barack Obama hails from Chicago, which we flew around, and we had talked about the campaign a fair bit over the previous days and during our flight. But as for Illinois? Not even a stop. Funny.

We had been flying into slightly rising terrain for a couple hours, and I re-marked on this to my brother. He snorted and said nothing. Looking around the very flat horizon, I could see that in the direction we were going the horizon had a raised, closer surface that receded down and had a further horizon beyond it if I looked out to the left or right. So I mentioned it again.

On the ground at KALO. Okay, Boss, I checked the oil and did a preflight, can I button it back up so we can make one more leg?

KALO tarmac. This one was the photographer's thought for the day...

He snorted again, "We've gained less than two hundred feet since Valparaiso." I had to look around and think about that a minute, then, "...it's still rising..."

Waterloo Regional Airport, in Cedar Falls, Iowa, is busy enough that it has been deemed controlled airspace, and we were going to be talking to the air traffic controller. I was a bit hesitant about that, as I'd been stumbling and struggling to remember what to say to a silent audience during the pattern flights at KVTA. Every leg of the pattern requires that a pilot announce their position and intentions. And as you approach an airport from outside the pattern, you do the same. That was challenging enough. Here, there would be somebody listening! Actually, there was somebody listening at KVTA as well, but they didn't usually respond. In this case, I knew we'd be needing to be saying the right thing. I was, frankly, intimidated.

When I asked about it, Quinn shook his head, then agreed to handle tower communications until I got a handle on the flying aspect. Actually, I don't think he even shook his head, but I felt like I was failing to superhumanly do everything at once that I needed to learn to do at once. Oh well.

Despite it being my first entry into controlled airspace, the landing was not particularly memorable. That is a lot better than the landing at KVPZ, where I had screwed everything up, though. We refueled and evaluated our options. We still felt we could tolerate more cockpit time and the weather continued to be comfortably VFR for the next few hours of our route. However, we didn't have a lot of daylight left, and we had both discovered that on long legs (flight legs, not human legs), our heels (the ones at the end of our human legs, but occurring specifically at the end of the flight legs) would fall asleep from sitting with the weight of our feet pressed back on them. Bizarre. But then again, I have really big feet, so I suppose they might be a bit heavy as well... things you learn in 3 hour flights in a little aircraft.

In the flight planning room at the FBO, we ruled out the next largest airport along our route, Sioux Falls, as being too far for us to make that day. We were hesitant to plan a stop at a really small airport, since we had no idea what lodging options or after hour services would be available to us at one of these smaller operations in case they closed before we arrived. So, we elected to deviate a bit south of course, flying almost due east to Fort Dodge, Iowa, KFOD.

We left Cedar Falls behind without so much as leaving the airport, and made the short trip to KFOD. Our landing approach as authorized by the tower was different this time, straight in for runway 24. After all the struggles of getting landings, these were a totally different kind of landing, but as it turned out I really liked it.

Whereas a normal landing pattern involves flying along parallel to the runway in the direction opposite the direction you intend to land, then turning and landing back in the direction you had just flown, a straight-in landing is exactly what it sounds like. I had miles of approach to intercept the glide angle on the lighted indicator that helps show whether you are in the vertical descent path that will bring you to the runway in a normal descent path. There are a number of different ones, each with its own special characteristics, but at KFOD we were intercepting a PAPI, or Precision Approach Path Indicator. I liked this long straight-in approach because after I brought us into the proper descent profile (according to the PAPI), I was able to stabilize at descent speed, and work on keeping the sight picture all the way down. I still didn't seem to have the final part figured out, but it was by far my best attempt to that point, and I felt like it was starting to make some sense. Quinn said I needed to get my landing sight picture down closer to the runway, as I was trying to flare too high, which was causing some of my problems. Okay, something to work on for the next round.

There were clouds moving in as we tied down the aircraft and headed in to look for some help in the FBO. They hooked us up with a courtesy car and helped us find a place to stay. We looked at the forecast, and the large mass of ugliness that was moving in from the Rockies was arriving outside even as we sat inside and looked at the weather forecast. Black clouds and a downpour arrived with gusto. Good thing we hadn't been trying to make it any further today. And the forecast for the coming day was not great for KFOD. Not terrible, but not great. Oh well.

We went out and started driving to find the hotel. The directions that we were given seemed really simple. But it was now pouring rain, and darkness had fallen while we gabbed with the FBO folks, arranged lodging, and checked out weather. So we were now in the middle of wet blackness on all sides. The headlights on our car did little that we could see to help us, it was so wet and dark out the only things that showed up were signs.

We were supposed to turn right immediately after the airport, but we were trying to see in the face of a moderate amount of oncoming traffic, whose headlights were also likely not helping them but from our view were beacons of near solar intensity in a blackness deeper than the darkest black. And so… we didn't see the turn. Pretty soon, we verified that we were in the middle of Fort Dodge rather than driving around it as intended. Quinn was driving, so now it was me navigating. I couldn't see the map without turning on the dome light in the courtesy car.

This was a problem.

The dome light resembled a small sun placed in the ceiling of the car. I'm not really kidding about that, it was a round white dome about six or eight inches across, a little miniature sun larger than any dome light I'd ever seen before. A sun even brighter than the headlights of oncoming traffic.

When the light was on, night vision was not only destroyed, but obliterated from memory. Driving in those conditions was probably not reasonable or safe, so I tried to get a sight picture of the map and then turn it off. After getting thoroughly lost a couple times in downtown Fort Dodge, driving hither and yon and back again, I eventually navigated us to the hotel where Quinn was able to denigrate my navigation abilities for the rest of the evening and into the following week. But we made it.

SECOND DAY

*In which endless horizons end, we are
overtaken by faster traffic (hard to imagine),
and we claw our way over the Black Hills*

When we got ready and headed out to the airport the following morning, the weather hadn't improved substantially. It was still pouring rain. We didn't exactly race to the airport, given how things looked, and when we did arrive our weather checks confirmed what we already knew. It really didn't look good. The ugliness that arrived after we did was still there, just like we were.

We got a thorough briefing on the weather along the route, and it looked like we were at the northern tip of the current ugliness. Weather was supposed to improve, and if it improved enough for us to take off we'd be free to go as far as we could make it that day.

Since we were hoping to reach Buffalo, Wyoming to visit some friends, and that was a long day away, we started by borrowing the courtesy car again and using our morning wait to visit a local breakfast restaurant and eat one of those too-hearty breakfasts that I rarely experience. Sometime during this face-stuffing exercise, I realized that after a whole life of hearing about it, I really was trying to get out of Dodge. And it wasn't working... yet...

Maybe if we were really stuck for the day we could look around and find the local historical society. For some reason that many of my travel companions can hardly abide, I am fascinated by museums, and I like to drag other people to them. Fort Dodge started, it would seem as a fort. But what happened then? Perhaps we could find out.

Or not. After waddling back out of the restaurant stuffed beyond bloating, we found ourselves looking at improving conditions. We took the courtesy car back to KFOD and found that weather at the airport had improved enough to become flyable, and was even better in the direction of our flight. The front that we had sat down in front of had passed over us as planned, and we were free to head out exactly as we had hoped. That, in the world of small craft aviation, is a small miracle.

So we took off, got out of Dodge, and headed across Iowa to try to make as much time as we could, with the hope of reaching Buffalo. We headed northwest to intercept the blue highlighter line we'd placed on our maps, in part because it would keep us along a major highway as we got beyond the patchwork of roads and fields into slightly less traveled country. But that intercept wouldn't take place until we were beyond Sioux Falls, so for the first leg we overflew Pocahontas airport (how cool is that?) and then skirted north of a couple of major fields of wind farms.

Wind farms are getting increasing exposure as we seek ways to generate energy without burning fossil fuels. From the air in a small plane, they can be quite intimidating. We were flying high enough to be above them, but they stick way up into the sky. Aeronautical charts (when you're in a plane, they're charts, when you're in a boat, they're charts, but on land they're just maps...) show anything that sticks up into the sky, and fields of wind turbines show up as a whole bunch of closely spaced vertical obstructions. Wind turbines are going up at a rate that is difficult for the charting offices to keep up with, but we elected to stay high enough and well away from anything that was a potential problem.

Impressive, though.

And a bit scary.

We flew over Paullina (never saw that name with two Ls before...) and Sioux Center, then started looking for a railroad that we were going to follow up to the highway. Except... we didn't find it. I hadn't yet seen a railroad from the air, so I'm sure I wasn't much help. Which is not to say we hadn't flown over other tracks, but I hadn't noticed them and did not yet have the search image in my mind. Eventually we were sure we had missed it, as we could see Sioux Falls off to our right ("Oh, by the way, we're in South Dakota..."), and we were monitoring their approach frequency.

We turned a little more north to try to intercept the railroad, and started looking at the little towns we could see. At one point, Quinn even asked me to fly over one of the towns so he could verify our location by reading the water tower! I, of course, gave him grief about that since he was our navigator.

We got our location sorted out, then intercepted the railroad ("Oh, that's what a railroad looks like."—"Well, yeah…") near Lennox and followed it, noting the little towns we were checking off on the map. Chancellor. Parker. Marion. Dolton. Bridgewater. Emory. Alexandria.

"Oooh! Mitchell looks really big after all those!"

We flew south of Mitchell, then followed I-90 west toward South Dakota.

I got a lot of practice crabbing. That doesn't mean acting grouchy (besides, I don't need any more practice at that, my wife tells me I'm an expert…). As the wind blows across the path of flight, the airplane has to fly a bit into the wind to maintain the track over the ground that you want. In this case, I was looking out slightly to the side ahead of us and watching as we slid along toward what would have been the eleven o'clock position instead of the twelve o'clock position straight ahead of us. This difference between the direction the aircraft is pointing and the direction it is heading is sometimes referred to as a crab angle… so I was crabbing.

As I prepare for the private pilot oral exam and flight exam (which is more commonly called a check ride), I'll need to practice calculating crab angles based on the speed the airplane flies, the wind speed, and the angle of the wind against the flight path. This allows flight by what's called dead reckoning, without continual reference to visual cues for location. In contrast, we were flying by pilotage, or visual references along our flight path.

As we kept tabs on our flight time, we started looking for a place to refuel and elected to stop at Chamberlain, K9V9. Except Quinn says it doesn't even deserve the K, it's so small. So it is just 9V9 to him. I haven't been able to verify its proper notation, I find it listed with and without a K…

As we approached the bend in I-90 where Quinn said the runway was supposed to be, there was nothing presenting itself. No runway whatsoever. I peered over at the map.

"Well, that looks like the bend just after Kimball… I think we haven't reached Chamberlain yet…" I was, unfortunately, right.

Of course, I never made future reference to this navigational error…

We flew over a large lake on the approach, which was a small lake on our chart. On the Omaha sectional, Red Lake was shown as a large dry lake bed with a small puddle in the center. But when we came to it, it was all water, rather a lot of it. I guess the drought is over…?

9V9 to KRAP. The Missouri River and some of the first terrain of the journey.

9V9 to KRAP. Vivian? Or Quinn? Or neither?

Then it was time for another straight-in landing, again with a PAPI to assist with determining the proper approach angle, but this time with a substantial headwind. Keeping the glide angle with a lower ground speed was a new twist, really, but again I had a long straight-in sight picture to work with and really felt like I was getting it. We floated above the glide path, then below it, but then got it stabilized and brought it down onto the runway. Was the landing beautiful? No, but it was a landing. I was still trying to flare too soon.

We back-taxied to the fueling area and had our first self-serve fuel experience. Thank goodness for self-serve. We never saw another soul at 9V9. According to the airport directory 9V9 is continuously attended. That may be, but I couldn't see any evidence of it. Of course, we didn't really need to bother anyone since the fuel was self-serve, so we didn't really try, either.

Next to the fuel area was a little house that straddled the airport boundary. It had a door that suggested a pilot lounge, so we went in and found a nice little room with a restroom attached to it. The rest of the house was private, according to the sign. The fact that there are occupied living quarters on the airport probably accounts for it being, "continuously attended." After using the facilities, we returned to the plane and flew out of there. Shortest visit of our trip, I think. We were grateful it was there, right when we needed it.

After taking off from 9V9, actually right after takeoff, while we were still just climbing out, we flew over the Missouri River. An impressive and mighty river, but not with the sort of beautiful characteristics at this location that the Mississippi had been displaying where we crossed it. In place of the forested banks and islands, with backwater areas and deep main channel, the river was a single main channel running through scrub lands. However, there was a nice little hint of terrain on the other side of the river that we were headed toward.

9V9 to KRAP. Badlands National Park out my window.

After the crossing, the earth flattened back out a bit, but not like what was behind us. We were starting to see more undulating terrain in general. As we flew along a straight course near I-90, still crabbing with the nose pointed a bit north of our track, we passed a couple of little towns of special significance to us. No, we didn't have any family roots there, nor had either of us ever visited these burgs. Instead, we just felt a particular affinity for their names. One was Vivian, which is the name of our grandmother on my mother's side. We were hoping to visit one grandmother on the trip, Grandma Rosie, but our Grandma Vickie lives in Arizona and we wouldn't get to see her on this voyage. But flying over her namesake village was a nice opportunity to think about her as we sailed along.

Not too long after, we flew in sight of Quinn, SD. Connection obvious. Maybe not quite the going concern he would have wanted to have associated himself with, but it seemed nice enough from our vantage point…

Along the line of travel we had laid out on the map, there was a clear need to stop at Rapid City, SD for fuel before starting across the mountains into Wyoming. Quinn added another reason to the importance of this stop. It seems he wanted to have the airport identifier in his logbook, so he could say he'd been to KRAP.

On the way, we passed just north of Badlands National Park. The terrain, that had been getting more and more interesting, became simply fantastic. Out my pilot-side window, we had some amazing views as we soldiered on toward KRAP, and Quinn tried to take a couple photos with his australopithecine (very old) digital point and shoot. I was carrying an even more outdated dinosaurian relic in my bag, a swing-lens panorama camera that uses (GASP!!!) film. But I was starting to think that bringing it had been sheer folly. I was simply too busy to ever pull it out of the bag. So I had to settle for opening my window for him to take the occasional photo.

I'd heard of the Badlands, of course, but I'd really never seen them or looked at photos. What a fantastic, almost lunar landscape. It sort of reminded me of a cross between the desert southwest and the Valley of Ten Thousand Smokes near my home. Very cool.

Pretty soon we were making contact with KRAP approach control. They had a Citation, which is a business jet manufactured by Cessna, due in and started talking with that aircraft soon after we had established contact. The controller told them about us because we were traffic that might be arriving around the same time, then switched over to ask us what sort of Piper we were.

Aircraft identify themselves by the tail number that is legally required to be displayed on the aircraft. All civil aircraft in the United States display an identifier that starts with N, and ours, as mentioned previously, is N624A. The N is omitted from radio communications, but the type of aircraft is included. We referred to ourselves as, "Piper 624 Alpha," since the Tri-Pacer was manufactured by Piper.

Since they abandoned the Tri-Pacer design, Piper has been making a lot of aircraft, some of which are pretty speedy little numbers, so apparently they thought we might be a much faster Piper of some sort.

My brother laughed, "Uh, we're in a PA-22, a Tri-Pacer, they'll be there well ahead of us, we're pretty slow…" I've since started referring to myself as Tri-Pacer 624A, because that way the controllers always know exactly how slow I am. Which is pretty slow. For an airplane. But then again it's a lot faster than driving a car…

Quinn was right, of course, about the Citation beating us to KRAP (better than having the KRAP beat out of us…). It was a bit unnerving (well, to me at least, I'm not sure anything ever unnerves Quinn…) because we had to wait quite some time knowing that the Citation was coming from generally the same direction we were and we couldn't see very well behind and above us. Eventually it showed up off to our left, though, and beat us in to the airport handily. We followed it in, with a long straight-in approach on runway 32. I definitely was liking these straight-in approaches. Though, again, it wasn't like the landing was anything to write home about. But that approach picture was starting to make sense to me, and I felt like it might come together some time.

We fueled the plane, looked at the time, and headed straight back out. We were a bit on the short side as far as time frame, since our friends in Buffalo had an evening church service we were hoping to attend with them, and we didn't want to make them (and by extension ourselves) late.

So we called and told them our estimated arrival time, and I admitted we hadn't really eaten since breakfast… could they bring sandwiches??? Actually,

KRAP to KBYG. Over the Black Hills, snow on the ground. "That looks cold." "Quit whining."

I said I was starving my poor brother and expected him to be hungry... Sheri laughed and said it was a crazy day, as her husband Albert had gone elk hunting that morning and she expected him to get in a bit bedraggled, too. But she assured us they would pick us up, sandwiches and all.

So off we went, and started the first climb challenge of the trip. We needed to climb up to get over the Black Hills. I'd heard of them too, but had no idea what they looked like, just like I had not known what to expect when we got to the Badlands. But the Black Hills were fairly impressive, they really looked like mountains to me in my little climb-challenged PA-22. Perhaps if you approach them from the west they look like hills, but seeing them after crossing the Midwest definitely made them look like mountains. In fact, I was looking at the chart to see what the name of the mountain range in front of us was, which is when I learned what they were.

We settled into the best climb speed and sat there all the way up the hillside, looking at the roads beneath us also climbing up and winding around through fields and trees and past the Pactola Reservoir. We managed to have about 1,000 feet clearance going over the top, which was better than I thought we were going to do for a while. I was amazed at the sheer density of roads beneath us. I had thought, looking at the wooded mountains on the way out of KRAP, that we would be looking at a whole bunch of road less wilderness, and was wondering whether we should be flying around more. But the map showed some roads and Quinn said we should make the straight path since we had good weather with ample ceiling, unless the airplane couldn't climb sufficiently or we had other concerns when we got a look at it. It turned out that there were roads visible pretty much the whole way across.

We attained an altitude of 7,800 feet crossing the Black Hills (and the South Dakota/Wyoming state line!), then settled in to cruise at 6,500 across Wyoming to Buffalo. The flight was fairly uneventful, skirting south of Keyhole Reservoir and Gillette. Past Gillette, we crossed over a set of wild looking hills that I would have to describe as crenellated. We crossed the Powder River, but were really looking for Crazy Woman Creek. Most of my life I had thought Crazy Woman Creek was a mythical place, but here we were, heading right over it!

Due to some unexplained defect in my character, I latched onto Louis L'Amour novels in sixth grade, and read them all. Then, I read them again. And then again. In fact, I still go through L'Amour phases. They are eminently readable and highly entertaining books. Although after a while there is a certain sameness... So I must also confess that I can't read too many in a row anymore. So long as you know that the good guy will win, will somehow impress upon the central lady character that she's the one for him without ever saying a word or actually courting her, and that he will have both a "knock-down, drag-out" fist fight and a gun battle to the death, you'll be well prepared for most L'Amour novels. Somehow, they can be fun despite this sameness.

All of which is a long way around (with me, everything is a long way around... just ask my wife...) to saying that Crazy Woman Creek is featured prominently in a L'Amour novel titled Crossfire Trail. A few years back, I was reading that novel and noticed that it featured an interesting geographical place name: Crazy Woman Creek. I was talking about it with Trevor, a friend of ours out in King Salmon who hails from Wyoming, and it turned out he was also a Louis L'Amour fan. Not only that, Crazy Woman Creek was a real creek, located right where he grew up. He had fished in it, hunted along it, and spent untold hours out there with his dad, none other than Albert, who we were on our way to visit (assuming he made it back from his elk hunt...).

So I had been made aware that it was a real place, but not only was it real, we were headed right over it on our way to Buffalo, Wyoming. The creek comes down out of the Bighorn Mountains, heading east, then passes south of Buffalo, and curves around and to the north as it joins Powder River, which is on its way to flow into the Yellowstone River. In the story, there are oil seeps near the creek where it emerges from the Bighorn Mountains, about ten miles south of Buffalo. We didn't fly down and look, so whether that is also real I can't vouch for... The source of the creek name appears to be up for debate, but no matter the origin it is one of the more colorful place names. Right up there with Up-A-Tree Creek, which is near where I live now... which I suspect relates to the bears in our area...

The other thing that stood out to me as we approached Buffalo was the Bighorn Mountains themselves. Trevor had mentioned them many times, and I'd heard of them. But I'd never seen them.

They are incredibly impressive mountains.

Whereas they could have been nice mountains at 8,000 feet high and met my feeble expectations, they loomed above Buffalo to a height of more than 13,000 feet. That's some serious looming. The snow cover came down fairly low, making them look very rugged in addition to their great height. They shadowed much of the valley, and we were glad it was still comfortably daylight and we had plenty of visibility to work with. I have to do some night flight to finish my private pilot training, but I'd rather keep it to the traffic pattern if possible… (author having conversation with himself… "Sorry Troy, FAA regulation says you have to make a cross country flight to a point more than 50 nautical miles away during night conditions in order to get your private pilot certificate…") or at least until I can get a feel for whether night flight is something I feel safe about.

Johnson County Airport, KBYG, sits on a nice little shelf above the town of Buffalo. We identified the airport easily due to its prominent location, advised other traffic of our intentions, and entered left downwind for runway 13, which was favored slightly by the existing breeze. So there I was, back to a pattern landing. Definitely not as smooth. More to think about, more to keep track of all at once. Probably the most difficult part is that the descent has to be started and stabilized before there is any glide path indication, and you have to execute turns during the descent phase.

There are some very good reasons why the traffic pattern is primarily close in, though. Originally, it helped to make sure the airplane was within gliding distance of the runway in the case of an engine failure. Engine failures are very rare in modern days, but it also helps to maintain situational awareness to construct a pattern of activity around the runway in the air. The defined legs of the pattern help traffic look out for each other, and it also allows a pilot opportunity to inspect the runway from the air before landing. As you can see, I'm trying to talk myself into liking it. And after I learn to do it better, I probably will…

I did manage the landing, though not a lovely one by any stretch. But it reinforced the benefit of having a good look at the runway and area before turning in. Amazing, in two days we had made it where we had hoped to make it in two days. That was the last time we were able to say anything like that on this trip.

But the trip was already shaking apart our assumptions about what we were going to manage to do on this voyage. For one thing, we'd faced a headwind on every single leg of the flight. Every. Single. Leg. I was starting to think that Tri-Pacer was synonymous with headwind, though Quinn said that west was the prevailing wind direction here. So yes, we'd made the distance we wanted to in two days. But we also found that we were doing so by flying substantially more hours than we had forecast. As we got to thinking about the long legs that we had planned through Canada, I started thinking those would not be feasible. Omak, Washington to Fort Nelson BC is well over 600 nm straight-line. Fort Nelson to Northway, Alaska is similar.

Uh oh... we were flying almost 8 hours to cover 550 nm where we were able to fly straight. Our next leg, to Omak, Washington, was 580 nm straight line, which we would obviously not fly in a straight line (those pesky mountains... what are they called? Oh yes! The Rockies!... they're too tall...), and none of the subsequent routes would be straight either.

Well, there would be enough time to worry about that later. At that point we were just intent on enjoying a night in Wyoming. Although Quinn had been grousing for a while about, "that white stuff. It's cold." I think this little refrain started over the Black Hills and persisted on and off all the way to Buffalo. Well, yes. Snow is cold. Seems he doesn't like cold. And he agreed to a flight to Alaska in October. I wasn't really sure if I should break the news to him or not... it was going to get a lot snowier... and colder...

Quinn had been taking great pleasure throughout our journey so far in folding the map (oops, did I say map? Of course I meant chart... we are in an airplane after all...). Every fold was a recognition of distance covered that we didn't have to cover again. A couple times, such as when we were approaching 9V9, he thought (hoped?) we were further than we, in fact, were.

He acknowledged that he was very much enjoying not only every chart fold, where he got to acknowledge our progress in some tangible way, but was loving every time we passed beyond a sectional (the name for an entire chart, which usually covers an area about the size of Montana, but in straightforward rectangles across the whole country). In fact, passing beyond an entire sectional was, "fabulous." And he greatly enjoyed disposing of sectionals we had passed out of. He wouldn't be using them again prior to their expiration (yep, they have dates on them, like pharmaceuticals or perishable food... but this time it's because they need to put new windmills and such on there...), and neither would I (though I love maps, and it hurt to see them get discarded... one of my friends later called the loss of the sectionals a "party foul"... seems I'm not the only one fond of maps...).

Quinn got to discard the Omaha sectional in KRAP, which he enjoyed inordinately, we were going to be passing out of the Cheyenne sectional soon after departing to the north from Buffalo, and he began to imagine how lovely it would be to discard the Billings sectional, since our route would take us in and out of the area it covered in relatively short order.

When I pointed out that it must be painful for a Lear captain to suffer through flight at the speed (actually, lack thereof) of a PA-22, he laughed.

"Actually, flying low and slow is part of the reason I thought this trip would be fun!" So, all that whining about our speed… apparently he was just having trouble adjusting himself to the reality now that he really was slow. We were almost never below 1,500 feet above ground level (agl), so I'm not sure that qualifies as low, but it does to someone that usually flies up in the flight levels (which are the altitudes at 18,000 feet above mean sea level and higher… territory of larger aircraft such as jets and turboprops for the most part…).

Anyway, the flat land was behind us. The great Rockies were our future until we got to Alaska, and any way you looked at it we would be doing mountain flying until we reached King Salmon. After all the endless horizons requiring dizzying scans, and thermals containing hawks at uncomfortable proximities, I was pleased to get back to a relatively wilderness setting with some mountain topography. It was more similar to where I am used to riding around in small planes. Doesn't make sense, as mountain flight is supposed to be more difficult and dangerous, but I feel more comfortable there. Go figure.

When Albert and Sheri picked us up, they took us down the road to town, stopping to wait for a herd of antelope to race across the road. Albert kept talking, as if nothing had happened. I was not so reserved… "Quinn! Did you see that?"

Albert laughed it off after we pointed it out. "Oh yeah, we have a lot of animals around here. In one field near our house I've seen as many as 250 mule deer in on some days."

"Excuse me? Did you say…"

"Yeah, it's pretty amazing."

"So, we heard you were hunting elk this morning. How'd you do?"

"Oh, yeah, we got back in there and got two elk down this morning, then cut them up and hung them. I have to go back in there tomorrow or the next day to bring out the meat."

Wow. I love hunting, but I'm basically one notch past rookie as an Alaska moose hunter. I can't even imagine shooting two relatively large animals, cleaning and quartering them both, and finishing all that within one day of work in time to pick up some friends at the airport. Amazing. Albert was a bit tired, it turned out (so he may be superhuman, but only moderately so…), but we enjoyed a nice evening. We met some friends of Trevor's, swapped some stories with Albert and Sheri, looked at Albert's rooms of trophies and generally shot the breeze. But it wasn't long before we all headed to bed so Quinn and I could make an early start to get on the road to Omak.

Well, in the sky to Omak, actually…

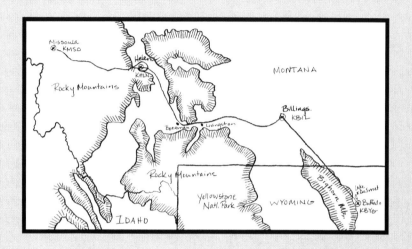

DAY 3

In which we are underwhelmed by our altitude performance, misjudge our location, and claw our way over much of the Rocky Mountains

The next morning we drove by the mule deer field on our way to the airport, and saw a measly 50 or 60 deer standing around (50 or 60 deer!!! All in one place!!! I've never seen anything like it, even when the deer population was booming where we grew up in Washington...). Then we watched two groups of antelope race around near the road as we drove up on the bench to the airport. Amazing. I was asking about hunting seasons, because when game animals are that plentiful they often start to become serious traffic hazards, and Albert suggested I come down and go hunting sometime. I could bring my son, Cedric.

We live where it is hard, slow work to hunt moose, and the odds of seeing one are usually pretty low. It almost seems as though hunting in a place like Buffalo would be more like harvest than hunt. Caribou hunting can be like that. Which I'm fine with, in principle, but I prefer moose hunting, for whatever reason. Maybe I just like doing things the hard way.

Albert dropped us off and we went into the FBO and asked to have the plane fueled, then walked out and found ... frost.

Uh, oh.

I had thought about getting wing covers for the plane, but hadn't gotten around to it, so here I was with my first reminder of what I should have done. I also hadn't purchased an engine heater, which seemed like it might become a bit of an issue. As I mentioned in regards to Quinn complaining about the snow and cold ... we were in for more cold. Especially in northern Canada and interior Alaska. And we were getting frost in Wyoming, which is so far south the season is way behind where we were headed. Hmm ...

We polished off most of the frost and waited for the sun to come up and work on the remainder. When it was clearly melting, we got some warm water and washed it all off, then hopped in and got ready to take off.

There was no discernible wind, but the dominant traffic was landing on runway 31, so we went that way to take off. The runway is 6,000 feet long, and at an elevation of 4,900 feet. According to our performance data in the Pilot's Operating Handbook (POH) for the airplane, that should be no problem. But we used an awful lot of the runway, probably 4,000 feet, and we were climbing incredibly anemically. Is this normal? Neither of us was happy with our takeoff performance, and Quinn started looking at our plans for the day.

Our next intended stop was Bozeman. Since it was similar in terms of airport elevation, we elected to change the plan and head to Billings, then Helena, so we could avoid airports over 4,000 feet. Having a little 135 hp Lycoming O-290-D2 engine in the airplane was a learning process. Most documentation is for the 150 hp or 160 hp Tri-Pacer configuration. Is this really all the little 135 hp can do? It did cruise at the listed book speed ... it just doesn't climb well. It might just have a cruise prop rather than a climb prop?

It turns out that one small detail we missed in the Airport/Facility Directory (AFD ... these acronyms never end, do they?) was that there is a slight slope to the runway. This meant that runway 31 was slightly uphill, making it the preferred landing runway in calm winds. However, the takeoff performance will be better from the downhill direction, so we could have had a bit better performance from using runway 13 (if these runway numbers are confusing, remember that the runway has a different name depending which direction you are facing ... runway 31 and 13 are the same stretch of pavement, just different directions ...).

I had another ongoing issue that Quinn was discussing with me on almost every takeoff.

"I'm going to have to glue your hand to the throttle, you keep wanting to take it off."

"It still feels weird to have only one hand on the yoke, I always want to put them both on there."

"Like I said, I'm going to have to glue your hand to the throttle."

Still, beyond my problems, we were pretty underwhelmed by the climb performance. We definitely noticed that the Short Wing Piper Club cruise climb recommendation of 90 mph was a better feeling climb than the Vy or Vx climb speeds.

We headed up toward Billings, and passed Lake DeSmet, home of the legendary "Smetty." The lake and its monster have a rather interesting and bizarre set of tales associated with them. Many lakes do, but especially for something only seven miles long, it seems a bit odd. Where we live, the legendary Iliamna monster seems more like it has earned its place since Iliamna Lake is so large it is virtually an inland sea, 77 miles long. And really, how would the various lake monsters actually have a viable earthwide population, when there is only one per lake? It does make one wonder how they breed. Perhaps they are also aviators, flying at night to rendezvous for a good old lake monster party. Another reason to be hesitant about flying at night... I bet they don't have navigation lights...

We worked our way up the valley toward Sheridan, and it wasn't long before the Cheyenne sectional was folded up for discard later. We passed over Sheridan and proceeded along the Bighorn Mountains, which loomed in the beautiful morning light to our west off the left wing. Wyoming was replaced by Montana beneath us when we weren't looking.

The visibility, which had been so great for our first miles, slowly deteriorated from 40 miles or more until we were looking into a light haze that made surface features difficult to ascertain even 10 miles out, though we could still see general horizon for probably 30 miles. Oddly enough, the National Weather Service assumes that 10 miles equals great visibility. That is the maximum visibility they report, at least that I've noticed so far, so the difference between 10 miles of visibility and 30 miles doesn't even register in their assessments of flight conditions. And 10 miles does represent great visibility, in comparison to five, or three. But after the previous day of 40 or more mile visibility, as well as the morning, it seemed like a pretty substantial difference.

Soon we were straining to compare the little patchwork of roads and the occasional stream below us with the sectional. We started to make out some roads, but were having difficulty deciphering which roads they pertained to on the map. We knew we were getting near the Billings airspace, so we called in to Billings approach control to let them know of our arrival.

Whoops! We were starting to see patches of the buildings emerging from the general featureless grayness of the surface, and we couldn't exactly tell where we were... but approach let us know that we were already well inside their 20 nm contact radius, and very high, even though we hadn't even picked out the airport yet. I spotted KBIL just as they were asking us if we knew where it was… a kind way for them to ask what in the world we were doing where we were… without having given them notice when we should have…

"My airplane."

"Your airplane."

Quinn took the controls and said he was going to do a forward slip to lose some altitude. A pretty impressive maneuver, and my first introduction to it.

In a slip, the rudder, which is the movable part of the vertical tail of the aircraft, is used to yaw the airplane away from the straight axis of travel. So whereas we had been crabbing along at an angle in relation to the ground when we were flying with a crosswind, a slip is a bit different. One difference is that a regular crab angle leaves your airplane in coordinated flight, which is to say that as a passenger it will feel fine, and if you aren't looking out the window you wouldn't know anything was happening.

In the airplane there is a little ball in a fluid-filled tube, which is one part of an instrument called a turn coordinator. The ball is heavier than the fluid, so left to gravity, it rests at the bottom of the tube. This is the condition of the ball when the airplane is sitting on level ground or in straight and level flight. If a turn is done in a coordinated manner, with just the right amount of aileron (the hinged portions at the trailing edge of the outer part of the wings) coordinated with just the right amount of rudder, the ball will stay at the bottom of the arced tube. However, if you don't match the rudder and aileron in a coordinated way, the aircraft will "slip," (or skid, but let's not get too confusing all at once…) offsetting the little ball in the turn coordinator. As I was about to find out, slips can feel very unsettling, not unlike driving too fast around a corner in a car.

Quinn turned the control column fully left, which would normally result in a hard turn to the left. However, instead of coordinating the rudder, he pushed in full right rudder. We were then looking out the left side of the aircraft as we slid down toward the ground sideways. The reason this maneuver can work is that the side of the aircraft works to increase the amount of drag, slowing the descent down.

Before the development of flaps, which are, like the ailerons, hinged surfaces at the trailing edge of the wings (though inboard, next to the fuselage), slips such as this were used to increase the descent rate of the aircraft for landing without increasing the forward speed. On most modern aircraft, flaps now are used to accomplish that same purpose, but demonstration of a forward slip to a landing is still part of the private pilot flight examination, and there are plenty of flapless aircraft still flying and in some places still being built.

The feeling of the slip was so startling that I found myself reaching to hold onto the cross brace across the windshield to alleviate the feeling that I might fall out of my side window.

Wow.

Both shocking and cool. I can't say I wanted to race out and do one myself right then, but I definitely got a full introduction to the maneuver.

Quinn proceeded to position us for a forward slip to a landing at KBIL, which he performed. He stalked out of the airplane and muttered, "talk to you inside."

Mildly alarmed, I followed him.

When we were in the FBO, Quinn told me he was actually pretty steamed with himself for getting inside their airspace without knowing where he was. He reminded me that to enter class C airspace you have to establish radio contact, which we had failed to do in a timely fashion due to our misunderstanding of our location. He and I had been debating which feature on the ground was what, and he'd guessed wrong about which stream on the ground was the one before the control perimeter. So far on our trip, we had only entered class C airspace at KRAP, and on that day we could see practically forever. There had never been a question about where we were. In approaching Billings we had been having trouble seeing clearly out at greater distances despite discerning the horizon far beyond. After kicking the topic around, we both agreed we had my little GPS on board, and there wasn't any reason not to use it, so we would make sure not to let that happen again. He said the controller was relatively kind not to make an issue out of it in this instance.

We fueled up and headed back out, taking off and following the highway toward Bozeman. Again, pretty anemic climb rate. Hmm...

And by the way... so long Billings sectional...

We were starting into the serious mountain flying now, and the winds were even more contrary. We needed to gain quite a bit of altitude for Bozeman Pass, and flying at best angle of climb and a good headwind we were moving pretty slow. Even after speeding up to fly at cruise climb, then finally cruise, we were lucky to make a groundspeed of more than 70 mph.

We wanted to get lots of altitude under us long before we got to the pass, but we found we had to descend to maintain cloud clearance in part of the route around Big Timber, and then labor to recapture the altitude before the pass. Flying into mountain passes with a headwind meant that the entire time we were needing to gain altitude we were dealing with air that was descending. We were flying an aircraft that is a pretty wimpy performer to start with, loaded to gross weight, and climbing in a downdraft.

I mentioned before that I really liked getting into the mountains and out of the plains, even though mountain flying has its own set of safety concerns. I was

KBIL to KHLN. Yellowstone River flowing through Livingston, Montana south of the airplane as we climb into a headwind, trying to get over Bozeman Pass to (where else?) Bozeman, after which we would head down the valley to Helena.

KBIL to KHLN. View ahead near Mission, Montana...we're in the mountains now...

getting a bit of a reality check now, as wind coming over the passes was stronger and downdrafts were prolonged and contrary. Over the plains, we got a bit of downdraft and a bit of updraft, but neither lasted long. While the mountain environment was more to my liking psychologically, it was certainly a challenge to deal with the realities of what the airplane could handle.

Despite all that, we managed to get back the altitude we needed, and had a fairly benign trip over Bozeman Pass into the valley that houses Bozeman itself. We overflew Gallatin Field, KBZN, and a regional jet called in as it was coming in behind us. It flew well out along our route of travel, then turned and came back in for a landing below us.

I was still a little unsettled about other craft in the same sky. But I managed to recognize that we had lots of clearance intellectually, it was just my kinesthetic senses that hadn't adjusted to this knowledge and caused me to gain 500 feet of altitude while the jet came in for landing thousands of feet below us.

Oops.

Quinn just shook his head and pointed at the altimeter.

We headed up the valley to Helena, where our next stop was. The weather was fine, and we had a great view of the entire valley of Canyon Ferry Lake out ahead of us. We passed off to the west of the Townsend Airport and watched and listened (and announced our presence) to a pilot doing touch-and-goes below.

As we continued on, we passed a couple miles east of a meaningless spot in a field that would attain significance six months later as the final resting place of Sparky Imeson, a renowned mountain flight instructor. Another reminder, no matter how much I like the mountains, that it is not a benign flight environment…

Leaving Canyon Ferry Airport off to our right, we continued along the lake. Finally, coming into the Helena area, we turned away from the lake and I had another opportunity for a long, straight-in landing at KHLN. Which was better. Not beautiful, but steadily better. I was rather pleased with the fact that I was improving with every landing. The hours of hashing over what I needed to do to improve that came between each landing was working in my favor. Quinn, on the other hand, got to spend hours getting interrupted by my random questions. "So, that landing back there, what was it again that I needed to do to make that come out better?"

"You needed to reduce power sooner to get your airspeed under control earlier."

"Right. So, when exactly should I be at pattern altitude and airspeed on a straight-in approach?"

"Well, just take the pattern and straighten it out. Your runway is how long? About a mile, usually, and the downwind leg is probably extended beyond that by a half mile or so. Then there is the base leg, which is likely in the range of a half mile, similar for final. So you are looking at around two miles minimum for the pattern altitude and descending portions of the pattern. If you can get yourself to pattern altitude earlier, say 5 miles out, you'll make the whole process easier by having a lot more prep time, so long as the approach path is safe to fly at that altitude."

Okay… remember all that… and ask again… and again… poor Quinn…

We spent a while getting updated weather. Our next target was Missoula, over the mountains. Beyond Missoula, there was a single spot, Mullan Pass, reporting IFR conditions on the way to Coeur D'Alene. We were thinking about the next leg, looking at the alternative of flying a slightly more northerly route out of Missoula that would take us through a wider mountain valley and dump us out near Sand Point.

In between taking turns with Quinn on the computer for weather briefings, I was looking around the FBO, which was deserted except for us. Clearly we were in firefighting country now. Every picture on the walls seemed like it was a fire or an aircraft fighting fire. Thank goodness there was no huge fire around when we were there. We got fueled up, wolfed down a candy bar and Coke (Mmmm… health food…), and headed back out.

We knew we were going to have a pretty short climb to get from 3,800 feet altitude on the airport to more than 7,000 feet in order to cross MacDonald Pass. On the way into Helena, we had passed by a ridge line along the side of Canyon Ferry Lake, and the wind was moving straight across from Helena to that ridge.

When the wind hits a ridge like that, it climbs up over it, so I started lobbying to head back over there and use that updraft to help climb. Quinn smirked, but said we could try it. Not sure what the smirk was about...

Again we took off and were somewhat appalled at the climb performance. It isn't that high here! And it's not warmer than ISA conditions! (Welcome to Tri-Pacer Land, where climb performance will never impress...well...anyone...) We circled back to the east a few miles to climb in the updraft, which worked really well and had us climbing the way we wished we could all the time. We then cut across the valley at 7,500 feet.

As we reached the center of the valley, we hit a major downdraft and gave up 500 feet of it pretty quick. Again, we were laboring to recover lost altitude flying into a headwind coming over mountains and going generally down. McDonald Pass is 6,300 feet, so we were hoping for 7,500 and not sure now if we were going to be able to get it. A few minutes later the plane started clawing back some of the altitude, so we were able to feel comfortable about our situation heading into the pass. My brother chuckled when he observed that after more than 30 minutes in the air, we were just passing the airport on our way across the valley toward the pass. Not exactly a Lear Jet. That probably explains the original smirk as well.

I had grown used to the sensation of my heels becoming a bit numb from having my big feet resting on them for hours at a time. I noticed on this flight that my left leg was itching a bit where it rested against the fuel tank selector, probably another little thing I would have to get used to just due to the combination of my large size and the airplane's small size.

After crossing the pass, we flew to Garrison, where the valley we had been flying along joined with the valley that I-90 had traveled up from Bozeman, and proceeded down toward Missoula. As we passed Rock Creek, the clouds started getting lower and lower, and we descended down past 6,000, then 5,000. Amazing how much more constricted a valley can feel as you set down into it like that. Maybe that's another part of the hazards of mountain flying... as you get down closer to the earth, the valley gets narrower and there is less room to maneuver.

We still had lots of room for a turn, but it felt close to me after all the time we'd spent trying to fly more than 3,000 feet above ground. Now we were a little less than 1,500 feet agl (above ground level) in a valley whose walls disappeared above us into clouds. It was both exhilarating and a bit claustrophobic. As we flew into Missoula, the clouds were higher in the valley around town, and it looked positively bright just north of us. Another long straight in landing at KMSO. I'm going to get it some day soon...

We had both spent the whole day being under-whelmed by our takeoff performance, and were thinking we ought to have the plane looked at. Before a flight, the engine is brought up to moderately high rpm in order to test how well it is working and diagnose problems ahead of time. With the brakes set, the engine is "run-up" to check how well the magnetos are performing and make sure the carb heat is working.

While most cars these days have electronic ignition systems, small aircraft are still operating on 50 year old technology to generate sparks for the spark plugs. The magneto transfers energy from the turning of the engine crank into a spark that is sent back to the engine to fire another revolution. Each of the cylinders is timed differently to maintain power through the entire rotation of the crank, making a sort of circular logic, but one that works. Each engine has two magnetos on it, which allows each cylinder to have two spark plugs on it. The spark plugs are located in a way to maximize the efficiency of the fuel burn, so the engine runs best when both magnetos are working. But the main purpose of the two magnetos is in case one should fail… the engine will still run though a little less efficiently.

During the run-up, the magnetos are tested by turning off one at a time and seeing how the engine rpm changes. The mag drop for our little beast was 125-175 rpm, which seems like a lot when most aircraft are supposed to be in the range of 75 rpm for the same test. But it's normal for the O-290-D2 engine we were flying behind, according to all the documentation we had found (which isn't always easy to come by, since the engine is no longer manufactured and hasn't been for, oh, let's just say a long time…).

We hadn't yet convinced ourselves that it was normal, despite what we read. And Quinn, having flown a number of other airplanes, was having a bit of trouble accepting the climb performance (really, the lack thereof...) of N624A, so we decided to have the spark plugs looked at. Aircraft fuel that is currently available is richer and has more lead in it than the fuel our engine was made for. Sometimes, engines running on this richer fuel develop lead deposits on the spark plugs, which reduces performance, so perhaps that was part of the problem. Quinn said he felt bad about calling it quits for the day when we had so far to go. I told him I thought that was funny since we'd been flying for pretty much the whole day, despite not traveling very far. We had been hoping to reach Omak, Washington and instead here we were, perhaps around halfway there from Buffalo, Wyoming. Welcome to small plane travel.

When Quinn looked at his watch he was a bit surprised. It was past closing time at Minuteman's (the FBO we were at) affiliated maintenance shop, unfortunately. So we asked for fuel and to have the plugs checked and oil changed in

On the ground at KMSO. Are we in Omak yet? Actually, no. We are in Missoula, a nice enough town, but we spent most of the day flying a ground speed of less than 70 mph.

the morning, then got some help finding lodging. The folks at our hotel sent a shuttle van out to pick us up, so we spent the wait checking the weather forecast.

Mullan Pass ceiling and visibility had been poor all day, and it seemed like it was expected to continue to be poor. But it looked from the data as though it really was a lone observation location, so there was no way to look around it and see whether it made sense in context. A single weather observation at that location in the mountains between Missoula and Coeur D'Alene is hard to make sense of when it differs from everything around it. And it wasn't precipitation, it just had crummy visibility and low ceilings. But there were no low clouds to the north or south of it in the mountains, or on either side.

We eventually decided the prudent thing would be to take the longer pass to the north. And by the way, where's our airport shuttle? The nice folks up at the front desk at Minuteman saw us looking out the window at airplanes landing and taking off and called to check on our ride. It had left for the airport some time before, so it probably was already here, somewhere. The front desk at the Holiday Inn Express was actually a bit mystified.

One of the FBO staff decided he knew what the problem was, and headed over to the passenger terminal and sure enough, the driver was over there waiting for us. While every airplane pilot on earth is familiar with the businesses at the airport that support civil aviation (basically everything other than airline flights), it is much less common for other people to be aware of that segment of the business. Including the shuttle driver. After gorging at the local Pizza Hut, we headed for bed.

I like to run. Some people would say jog, since I'm not very fast. While I was in Columbus I had run a few times, ranging from six to fourteen miles (okay, I don't just like to run, I run marathons and am therefore crazy and think nothing of runs over ten miles… so sue me…). I had shipped all my running gear home and was committing to no runs for the duration of the flight. Mostly just due to the fact that we were planning on using all our daylight for flying, but also because we didn't have a lot of payload in 624A. So why am I telling you this? Good question, I can't remember. Oh, wait, yes, I was just pointing out that I should have been physically rested due to less exercise than normal. But in fact, I was exhausted at the end of every day. I would fall asleep at some ridiculous time like 8 or 9 PM (okay, I'm usually a bit of a night owl as well…), then wake up at 3 AM and be unable to get back to sleep for a couple hours. Learning to fly is hard work!

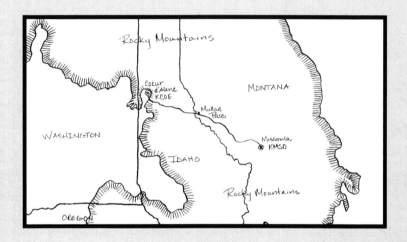

DAY 4

In which we spend the entire day sitting in the KMSO Minuteman FBO while the airplane gets some TLC, then make a late and hasty dash over the rest of the Rockies

The next morning, Quinn went out to taxi the airplane to the maintenance shop and explain to them what we were hoping to have them do. Before firing it up, he came back in and asked me to come out and look. The fuel selector valve had blue streaks running down from it and into the wall upholstery. That's odd, we never smelled fuel. I checked my pant leg where I had felt the itch the previous day, and there was a small round circle of blue. Just a tiny bit, but it looked like fuel had leaked onto my pant leg and evaporated. So I apparently won't be dealing with an itchy leg on every flight. Another job for the maintenance shop. I hope they didn't get around to filling it last night …? "Yes, it was filled last night right after you requested it!" D'Oh!

The folks in the shop labored away, draining the fuel, pulling off the fuel selector valve and replacing the newly leaking gasket. They checked all the spark plugs and found two that functioned very poorly, replacing them with new ones. But when they did a follow-up test of the mags, the rpm drop had not improved.

They decided to check the mags, and found that one of them had been almost completely melted down inside. They were surprised it worked at all!

Quinn had flown the aircraft up from Texas after we bought it, and found a mag was cutting out on him at one point, but then it resumed normal operation. He stopped and had it checked, at which time it was working fine, so the shop mechanics thought perhaps some condensation had been in the leads but had been burned out by the engine heat during flight, and now it was fine.

Well, apparently not.

The mag had definitely had some serious problem at some point. So they went ahead and rebuilt the failing mag for us. The mag drop was still not changed much, but some potential weak points had been dealt with, so that was good. And there was no metal in the screen, which was also good. The screen is a precursor to modern oil filters, and is primarily able to catch metal shavings. Metal shavings in the oil mean the engine is shaving pieces of itself off... a very bad situation which we were happy we weren't in. It means the engine needs overhaul before it can be flown again.

So we didn't have that sort of trouble, our spark plugs and magnetos were in better shape, and the fuel leak was fixed. The mechanic that brought the plane out to us wished us well and sent us away... after having us sign a blank receipt for the repair.

"Cute plane. When you get it home, you should have the exhaust looked at."

Check, that was what the last guy said too...

I had started to expect everything to come back with small problems, and was crossing my fingers against large problems at this point. Old airplane buyer's syndrome... a certain nervous tick.

We had borrowed a courtesy car to run grab some lunch, but other than that we had spent the morning and afternoon sitting in the FBO watching airplanes out the window, reading magazines, and talking. The magazines were interesting. It was obvious that most of the flights the FBO catered to were business jets or turbines. At least, that appeared to be the business model. The waiting area was filled with magazines talking about owning, operating, and riding in business jets, as well as sales literature and marketing for all sorts of business aircraft. Much of it seemed fairly irrelevant to my life, but still entertaining as I tried to understand the finer points of one multi-million dollar aircraft over another.

There were two aircraft that made repeated flights while we waited. One was a little Piper PA-18, generally known as a Super Cub. Super Cubs are made of welded steel tubing with fabric stretched over it, have two seats, one in front of the other, and have wings up high like our Tri-Pacer. In fact, our Tri-Pacer is a basically similar design in which the wings are a bit shorter and the main cabin has been stretched sideways to accommodate side-by-side seating in both front and back. But Super Cubs have the third wheel hanging under the tail instead of out on the nose of the aircraft. The main gear with the two primary wheels are moved forward, and the configuration is referred to as a taildragger.

Taildraggers are the iconic backcountry aircraft, and the Super Cub is probably the most iconic of them all. Though very small, they can fly very slow, which means they can land and takeoff in very short distances. They can haul a pretty respectable load for a little two-seat aircraft, and are the vehicle of choice for many people trying to access the wilds of Alaska. Put a pair of huge balloon tires on them and you can land in places people wouldn't think of landing with something like our Tri-Pacer, with its little tires, tricycle gear (that front tire isn't helpful with rough terrain, it just makes ground handling easier on good surfaces like runways), and shorter wings. The flip side is that the Super Cub is not able to fly very fast under any scenario, so it is a poor aircraft for cross-country travel.

The gentleman flying the cub even looked like a bush pilot. He wore jeans and a T-shirt under a light cotton jacket with tennis shoes and a baseball cap as he strolled in and out of the building to and from his plane between flights.

This was a little different from the gentleman flying the second plane. He wore chinos, a button-down shirt, and sunglasses and carried a briefcase as he went to and from his plane, a Cirrus SR-22 Turbo.

Cirrus is a relatively new aircraft company, and they aren't likely to show up in any numbers in Alaska. But they have sold many, many aircraft in the contiguous states by concentrating on the opposite market segment. The SR-22 does not take off in a short distance. Nor does it land in a short distance. Well, I suppose it does compared to some aircraft, but in comparison to the cub it takes up four times as much room or more for landing and takeoff. It has small landing gear with a nose wheel, wings down low, is made of molded composite pieces, and flies at 200 miles per hour while carrying four people. A really great cross-country aircraft, but hopeless for backcountry flight.

I told Quinn it looked like a yuppie airplane, which I think may have slightly offended him… (he likes fast, low-wing, cross-country airplanes… I suppose that's okay…).

I also asked Quinn a million questions about turbine engines since there were all sorts of turbine-centered magazines laying around. He got out a paper and drew a turbine engine for me, explaining how it operated. The concept is very interesting, it is basically a big flame-driven fan. He drew it out, complained about his own lack of drawing talent, then proceeded to illustrate exactly every stage of its operation. A few minutes later, I found a diagram of a turbine in one of the magazines. It was exactly the same as his drawing… if only I was that good at the things I'm not good at! Every kid is a great artist and singer, but by the time we reach adulthood we tend to have put those talents aside as something we can't do... sad, really. So my new revelation about my brother Quinn? He could be an artist. He just doesn't think so.

The huge maps on the wall in the hallway of Minuteman were practically worn out from me going and measuring mileages from one place to another. The map wall was very impressive, the most complete map layout of any FBO we had been in. We noticed the mountains throughout the route ahead of us. We were definitely in for some extended mountain flying. We also noticed that the mountains up in northern Canada were pretty high!

"I thought you said that after we got through Montana we wouldn't have to fly this high again," Quinn complained to me.

"Well, I didn't think the airfields were that high up there, but I didn't really look... are they?"

Actually, the airfields we were headed for in Canada weren't particularly high, but there were definitely some pretty good mountains along our route of travel up there. Especially as we passed in the shadow of the second-highest mountain in North America, as well as some of its junior attendants, on our way into Alaska. We checked the weather repeatedly during the wait. I also started checking the daylight, as I was getting concerned about our ability to get out of town in time to make it to Coeur D'Alene before dark.

When the mechanic finally brought the plane to us, we were getting going at 4:30 PM. We had been obsessively checking weather all day, and Mullan Pass was fine despite the previous day's poor forecasts, and we had daylight to get to Coeur D'Alene (barely) so off we went.

We hadn't been in the air too long and I knew that we were going to be arriving pretty late. The headwind continued, and of course it was greater, not less, than we had anticipated. According to our GPS, we would be arriving after civil twilight, which is pretty dark. But the clouds were well above the mountain tops, the sun was shining at a gloriously low angle, and we had good visibility. Quinn was satisfied with the timing so we proceeded on. Me? I'm a chicken, I would have turned around. I hear it gets dark at night.

Other than the now-expected headwind, the flight went fine. Early in the flight, there are two parallel valleys that depart from the Missoula area. I looked at the one that was north of the highway, but common sense kept me over the emergency landing surface... I mean highway... and we soldiered on, squinting into the sun. The plan of heading north the long way to avoid Mullan Pass was discarded in the face of good flight conditions in the pass, so other than noting the entrance to that route soon after takeoff we never gave it a second thought.

KMSO to KCOE. View northwest after departing KMSO.

KMSO to KCOE. Lolo National Forest along the Clark Fork.

KMSO to KCOE. Interstate 90 crossing the Clark Fork west of Huson.

KMSO to KCOE. Sunset over the Rocky Mountains on the way to Idaho.

I did think about my camera stowed away in the back seat, though. The view was entrancing, and as the sun dipped below the horizon the clouds were lit up above us and visibility continued to be good as the evening light illuminated the long, narrow valley ahead of us. The wooded slopes were not as rocky or abrupt as some we had passed, but the road wound through some narrow spots. We solved the riddle of the Mullan Pass visibility when we observed smoke rising from an area a little bit south and west of the pass; a forest fire had been filling the valley with smoke. No wonder the report didn't make sense with what we knew about cloud cover... it wasn't due to cloud cover at all!

The smoking burn area was one of the last things we saw before the sun went down and the world became still very visible, but shadowed. We turned on our nav lights and beacon, and headed off down the valley. The visibility was actually quite good though, largely due to the highway beneath us. We could see Coeur D'Alene off in the distance from the lights, and the highway lights below leading there as clear as day. We flew into Coeur D'Alene, here it was, my first night landing. And a pattern landing, at that.

The pattern went okay, for a change, then base and final. Everything looking pretty good. Here comes the runway, pull back...

"Not so fast!!!!" Quinn said, sounding rather urgent.

Then we fell out of the sky.

...

...oops!...

...

It was probably only six or eight feet, but it was my hardest landing. What Quinn had been trying to convey to me, in the half-second after I had already screwed up, was not to pull back so fast. As I said before... oops. And I had been doing so well!

"I didn't warn you appropriately about the differences in landing at night instead of during daylight. You need to keep a reference way down the runway, not near the plane."

Quinn got out to inspect after we parked, and wasn't sure whether I had done anything truly problematic or not. The gear was a bit cockeyed looking, but we had just turned hard left to pull into our parking spot. When we moved the airplane back and forward, it straightened right up. Anyway, it was a hard landing, so we needed to have the plane inspected. Unfortunately it was Friday night, so getting somebody to check the plane out was going to be a bit of a challenge. And it would be a challenge for Saturday...

Meanwhile, KCOE, also known as the Coeur D'Alene Airport—Pappy Boyington Field (that's really its name! Pappy Boyington was a World War II ace from the area), was dead (the field, not Pappy Boyington… although come to think of it I believe he's also dead…). There was no sign of anybody. Thank goodness for cell phones. But who was I going to call? Ghostbusters? I had no phone book, no local intelligence about the area.

So, I did what any reasonable person would do. I called my wife. She, after all, has a computer attached to internet, from whence all information we needed could be gleaned… She called back a few minutes later after coming up with a hotel near KCOE.

I thanked her, then called the hotel. They did not have a shuttle service, and seemed confused about which airport we were coming from. "That would be about 45 minutes by taxi."

"Really? I thought you were right near the airport?"

"Well, the airport is in Spokane, and we're over in Hayden, Idaho."

"Right, you're in Hayden near the Coeur D'Alene airport."

"You mean you're at the little airport here in town…?"

But they still didn't have a shuttle. They rounded up a number for us to call for a taxi, which I did, and then we found our way to the parking lot and waited in the pleasantly cool local air. Not bad for October. At least in King Salmon, it would be lots colder. Then I spent the night fretting about how to get the airplane looked at.

Becky tells me that fretting doesn't actually accomplish anything, and she's right.

But I did it anyway.

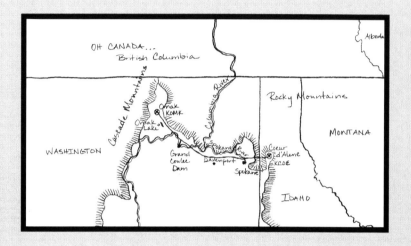

DAY 5

*In which we travel less far than we hoped but
are glad to have stopped where we did*

The next morning I started looking for a mechanic to come and look at the plane. I started by calling the FBO as soon as they opened. I really did not want to be on the other end of the phone. "Hi, I know it is Saturday, but I had a bad landing last night and I have a long way to go and I'm hoping you can come look at my plane and fix anything I might have broken...?"

Actually, they were all really nice, and it seemed as if everybody we encountered was interested in our project. However, the FBO didn't have a mechanic on staff, and the name they gave me was for a gentleman that was busy using his weekend to work on his farm. It was the only lead they had, though, so I called him anyway. There was no answer, so I left a message. His wife returned the call a few minutes later, just as I was trying to evaluate my options (...okay... freaking out...), and said he wasn't available, but I did get another phone number out of the deal. The number I called next was for a gentleman that also wasn't answering the phone, but I left another message and fretted.

I mean, waited.

He returned my call shortly, from a hangar just down the way from our airplane. He had been out flying his cub, and was happy to go down and look over 624A for us. He told me ahead of time that he'd be surprised if we had done any damage based on my description.

"The landing gear on those things is freakishly strong."

Quinn sounded pleased with that, "What exactly were his words? Freakishly strong?"

Actually, in retrospect, perhaps he just sounded amused.

The mechanic reported back in short order that it looked fine, though we might want to have some of the sheet metal work on the belly redone. Another project to go with the exhaust.

We packed up and went to load the plane, settled up with the mechanic, and asked for fuel. The ladies at the FBO looked at each other… then looked back at me…

"Well, we mostly sell Jet-A, but we can fill it with 100 low lead if you want…"

"So… if you were me, would you ask you to fill the plane?"

"No. If I were you I'd go use the self-serve across the field."

"Okay. Done. Thank you very much."

So that is exactly what we did. Airplane fuel used to be widely available in a variety of octanes and lead treatments. However, most fields now offer only one variety of aviation gasoline, which is 100 octane with lower lead content than the other 100 octane aviation fuel that used to be available. The 80/87 and the 110 octane fuels are basically impossible to find now. Our little airplane was designed for using the 80/87 octane fuel, but we could run it on 100LL, so that was what we did. However, jet and turbine engines do not use gasoline, they use a specially formulated kerosene, or diesel, fuel, which is called Jet-A. The FBO we were at was primarily set up for serving the higher-end aircraft that came in. Which we definitely were not…

The phase-out of leaded fuel for aircraft has been hampered by the lack of manufacturing research. Since so few people fly planes, the market for aviation fuel is not great. So there isn't much financial incentive for companies to develop a better or newer fuel. At the same time, most engine designs in service make use of the higher octane to produce more power, and are not built to run on lower octane fuels. So while some airplanes were made for a low octane fuel, many were not. Those that were designed to run on the 80/87 aviation fuel can usually be altered to make it feasible to operate them with automobile fuel. This has been done for ours, so in principle we could fill up at the corner Chevron station. If we could land and taxi there, anyway… (I think the letters to the editor that followed that incident would be pretty entertaining). But most piston aircraft are stuck using a legacy fuel with tetraethyl lead that the EPA is increasingly uncomfortable authorizing for continued use. Now, there is some movement afoot, and perhaps the future of aviation fuels will be addressed soon with a couple new entrants to the market. The affordability of those fuels will be interesting to see, but it is great that they are being developed.

Quinn and I grew up in Omak, Washington, and were on the west side of the Rockies primarily because we wanted to visit the home we see only rarely now. Our original intent had been to spend a night (or maybe two?) there and visit friends and relatives, as our third stop, coming as it would have after Buffalo, Wyoming. Of course, we flew six hours from Buffalo and made it only to Missoula. We had flown only one short flight from Missoula and then another night in Coeur D'Alene. So we were two nights behind our imagined time frame, plus the additional Monday night we lost back in Columbus before ever starting.

So we were starting to think about making as much distance as we could now, given the slowness of the first portion of our trip and the creeping sense that the weather was going to shut us down at any moment. But we called ahead so our grandmother and aunt could know we were coming, as both Quinn and I had hoped to stop and visit. Ninety-three year old grandmothers with hearts of gold are rare, we really wanted to say hi.

After fueling up at the self-serve, we followed a parade of GA airplanes taxiing for takeoff. One gentleman was taxiing in a bit of a strange weave, and didn't know where to go. It was reassuring to see somebody else ask for help. I wasn't the only clueless flyer out there.

Quinn helped him with taxi directions to get to the runway he wanted, and we filed along behind him, as we were headed for the same runway. While taxiing, we got a look at an RV that was doing pattern work. My brother is contemplating building an RV, and he was mooning over it as we watched it go by. It did look nice, but he really likes them because they're fast, and because he'd like to build his own airplane. They are built from kits by people who have a desire to spend five years putting their airplane together. I wasn't quite that patient...

We took off from KCOE and headed west, north of Spokane. Over Newman Lake, we watched a couple planes below us heading back toward KCOE, then called in to Spokane and requested VFR flight following. I was still hazy on the nature of the different flight following and air traffic control processes. I had a book understanding sufficient to pass the written test, but I was a bit overwhelmed with flying the airplane, so Quinn was still handling radios for controlled airspace.

We passed over some farms amid trees north of Spokane over Colbert, WA, then over a wooded knoll with a few dirt roads here and there on it. I was spending part of my scan time learning how to keep an eye out for an emergency landing site. Some of those dirt roads looked like they might work fine, but some of them were so narrow or winding that they looked to be no help in an emergency. I loved looking around while I was flying, but I was still struggling to divide my attention appropriately among the important tasks. Airspace around me, instruments, radio chatter, emergency landing options. Repeat. Again. And again.

After cresting over the knoll, we came into sight of the Spokane River. What a beauty. I had driven to Spokane many times, and I could see the road we drove on down to the south, but I hadn't ever really had a good look at the Spokane River other than where it runs through downtown Spokane. The sheer size of it surprised me. Of course, the occasional dam makes it even a little larger... The towns on the familiar road looked so close. Yet Davenport, Wilbur, and Creston are surrounded by wheat fields and sit among gently undulating hills. There is no sense when you are driving through them of the nearby huge gash in the earth filled with water, or of wooded hills on the other side of that unseen river. From up in the air, the road looked as if it was crossing completely flat country.

We stayed north of the river to where it joined with Lake Roosevelt, looking below for emergency landing sites. More dirt roads wound through the trees beneath us, offering spots with sufficient clearance for an emergency, but across the river were better options because the roads didn't have trees hemming them in. I hadn't yet thought through all this at the time, but it becomes very important to know the glide rate of the aircraft... if the engine fails, how far could I make it? If our altitude allowed, it would have been better to glide across the water to the easier landing side. Just another of a long list of things I needed to learn.

When we reached Lake Roosevelt, we followed it to Grand Coulee Dam, flying almost directly over the lake. Having grown up nearby, I had seen the dam frequently from the road with its stark beauty. I had toured the inside of the dam as a kid, where we heard about it being the largest concrete structure in the United States, the largest dam on earth (a title I believe it no longer holds), and being built to include survival bunkers inside (for what eventuality, I wonder?). I had seen water spilled over the spillway and light shows on the spilling white water foam at night for entertainment. I had driven over the dam, back in more trusting times when people hadn't begun to blow things up with vehicles full of fertilizer or fly into things with aircraft acting as fuel bombs. I think if you tried to drive over it now it would be an arresting experience...

The only thing I hadn't done was run the Over the Dam Run, a 10K race that included running over the dam itself. Perhaps some day I'll mark that one

KCOE to KOMK. Flying over Lake Roosevelt after passing Spokane.

KCOE to KOMK. Lake Roosevelt is a huge lake created by the Grand Coulee Dam on the Columbia River. It seemed like we were flying over it for a long time. Because we were...

off the Grand Coulee Dam life list. But the 2009 race was canceled, so perhaps that window of opportunity has closed in the new focus on limiting access to potential terrorist targets.

Up above the dam, I was getting a whole different perspective now. The contrast between the two sides of the lake was stark from up above, with the wooded north and the fields on the south. While the wooded north is mountainous, the mountains are rounded. It is a lovely, but somewhat gentle landscape... until you get to the river. The river cuts down into a bedrock chasm that stands in sharp contrast to the gentle terrain on either side. The rock walls on either side of the dam rise from below the dam to well above it, sheer gray walls standing nearly vertical against a horizontal world on either side. The road from Spokane is carved into this wall, running down to the town of Grand Coulee Dam at the base of the dam. Now I assume the odds of the dam failing are very low. But looking at the town and then at the huge wall of the dam holding back all that water above seems a bit ominous. I just really wouldn't want to be looking up at a wall like that knowing that what lay behind it was enough to wipe out everything around me... including me...

When driving from Spokane to Omak, we would have gone a bit north into the Colville Indian Reservation and crossed Disautel Pass, coming into Omak from the east. Rather than fly that same route, we headed a bit down the river, then up across the Omak Lake basin, a big basin that appears to be left over from the ancient Lake Missoula floods.

A few times as a kid I went there to go swimming. It is a closed basin, with no outflow, and the water is strangely alkaline to taste. Most closed water basins collect salt, but whether Omak Lake is salty I don't know. The overwhelming sensation from tasting it is chalk. On this day, with a few thin clouds high above, it was as pretty as a picture from 4,500 feet. As we approached the end of Omak Lake, we had a good view of the town and the Okanogan River Valley.

This section of airspace is designated as a military operations area, or MOA. That can be a serious concern for someone in a small, slow aircraft. Military flights are often at a high rate of speed and the see-and-avoid principle becomes functionally impossible at that velocity. However, the Okanogan MOA was not in use, so we cut across it without fear of fighter jets. Interesting that, until planning for this trip, I had no idea that there were military operations in that airspace, despite living beneath it...

I started my descent while still over Omak Lake, trying to accomplish all the things I needed to in a timely fashion. I always thought of Omak Lake as being a long way out of town. Flight is quite a bit different in many respects, but the speed of it can catch you by surprise sometimes. Here we were flying a relatively

KCOE to KOMK. Omak in the distance in the Okanogan River Valley, coming home for a short visit.

slow airplane, and when we were miles away we were preparing to pull in the driveway. Well, sort of, at least in a certain aeronautical sense...

It was amazingly easy to find the airport when I already knew where it was! We lived a mile from the runway (by straight line) for my entire growing up years. I was surprised now by how close in it seemed. We were flying over Omak, which is down in the Okanogan River valley, preparing for landing at KOMK, which is up on the Pogue Flat above the valley, and we were only three miles out.

Somehow, three miles doesn't seem very far when you are up in the air. In fact, it seems like very little. All those VFR minimums in regulation (rules about how much clearance from clouds, how much horizontal visibility, and how much vertical distance between cloud ceiling and ground are required for VFR flight) were taking on a whole different meaning now that I was getting a chance in the air to see what the distances were. Three miles visibility seems pretty close in. Let alone one mile for the least restrictive airspace near ground level around rural areas. Three miles looked like it would feel awful close in to me.

"Slow down, keep descent rate under control, aim for the numbers." We lined up for a straight-in landing again, which brought us right over land I'd seen many times. But as interested as I was in getting a better look, I found that I did not have time to gawk. Landing was getting better, but the idea of seeing something other than the runway during the approach was still laughable. I think we must have flown right over the farm I grew up on, or at the very least it would have been right out my window, but I didn't see it. But I had a really good long look at the runway all the way in. This translated to another almost successful attempt.

I was only making one landing every couple hundred miles, but by golly it was starting to work. I was still terrified of the thought of solo flight, but could now imagine that the day would come when I was actually ready. That was definitely progress. And here we were, Saturday noon at the town we grew up in. There was no sign of activity at the airport, but KOMK isn't exactly an international airport, so that wasn't totally surprising.

We taxied to the self-serve station and filled the tanks, and I tried to call my aunt and grandmother. No answer. Since we basically flew right over their house, I thought they might have seen us and started on their way... and sure enough we had barely finished fueling up and here they came. We showed them the little fabric and steel contraption we'd been traveling in, and they looked it over.

"Must be pretty tight in there."

"Well, yes it is, actually. But we're still talking to each other... most of the time."

Grandma Rosie and Aunt Rosie had lunch waiting for us back at their house. We felt like we should put some distance behind us, but we could certainly do with some food. And I had been thinking about a couple things that I was hauling in the back of the airplane... they really didn't need to be there. I wasn't going to be taking any photographs. I was realizing that as a fact. I also didn't need all my clothes. I had extra stuff that I was sure I could pare down to save weight. So I went and grabbed my bag, Quinn taxied the airplane over to tie it down, and we went to lunch.

We enjoyed our visit and let lunch stretch on for a while, as this moment was one of the major reasons we chose the route we did. Then we got to looking at each other... and Quinn said, "at this point, we aren't going to make it very far into Canada today anyway, so why don't we just stay."

I was a hard sell. I said, "Okay."

I packed up a bag to mail home, saving us what was probably only fifteen pounds, but it felt important to try. Probably the first of many futile attempts to make a slow plane fly faster, but at least I did what I could. The symbolic value of putting the camera in the bag to be mailed was probably the most important. I had somehow imagined that I'd be flying along and have all this time to focus on other activities. The realization that flying was a full-time occupation when you are in the air had finally arrived in my rather slow consciousness.

We got to hang around and visit one of my cousins and her family. I played a mean game of dodgeball with one of my nephews, in which the rules and the score continuously and mysteriously changed, but only in his favor. After multiple games of questionable outcome, I was done but he was not. Sadly for him, he couldn't rustle up another game with anybody else.

We called our friend Greg and invited ourselves to stay at his house, as there was no room at our aunt's place. Before heading up to his place, we went to one of my favorite little restaurants, the Breadline Café, for a nice dinner with Aunt Rosie and Grandma Rosie. Afterward, we went back to the airport to get the rest of our stuff and went on to Greg's house, where we sat around their living room and spent another few hours visiting.

I was initially dismayed to find that they no longer had a guitar in the corner. I keep threatening to buy a guitar and leave it at my parents' house. Mom seems to feel that it would take up too much space. But Greg had a guitar in the corner last time I was there so I was looking forward to sitting around and playing some. Quinn doesn't have a guitar at his house either, so I hadn't touched one for two weeks now.

I got over my disappointment easily enough, because it really is a minor thing. I was sure I could survive another night without playing around on a guitar. I don't play well anyway... I just like it. We were playing three-way catchup with their family and each of ours, and Greg invited his parents and his brother Justin over to the house. Pretty soon Justin showed up with... a guitar!

"Greg said you needed to play this for a while."

Wow! Talk about pressure! He brings a guitar and an audience (Justin is quite an accomplished player)! So we talked some more, and I plucked my way around a few songs, ate dessert, drank coffee, did all of the nothing that you do when enjoying a visit with old friends.

Greg's parents came over to say hi as well, and we packed a lot of visiting in. After visiting as much as we could, we found we were all yawning so we headed to bed. And to think we might have missed all that to make two or three hundred miles into Canada and stay in some random motel somewhere. Still, that is the sort of trade off you have to weigh when you are in an extremely weather-limited conveyance on a time-limited trip.

DAY 6

*In which we surprise ourselves by traveling
farther than on any other day of the trip with
perfect weather and tailwinds ("Don't look now,
but we're going faster than our airspeed.")*

The next day dawned while we were packing ourselves in Greg's car to
go to the airport. We drove by our old home on the way. The previous evening as we drove past it in the dark there wasn't much we could see. But in
the early morning, there it all was. But different. The pastures looked like they
had been grazed down more than when we lived there, but perhaps most of all
it was just as though looking at my own past through a slight haze. I couldn't
help but think about all those years of farm work and life. Funny how much
I miss it still.

The farm was 140 acres of freedom to my brothers and me. We had grown
hay on one corner of it, had seen some areas of it as apple orchard for a few years
before the orchards were taken out for pasture, and raised animals. The animals
were primarily cattle and horses, but occasionally we would make a go at chick-
ens, pheasants, pigs, or some other novelty. We also had untold numbers of cats
and a dog or two running around the entire time we lived there.

The airport was so close that we always saw air traffic as it came and went. I was pretty oblivious to the air traffic though. It had not occurred to me when somebody flew over that I might know them. Especially when I was really young, the highest thoughts I had were up in the elm trees we tried to build forts in, or the cottonwood tree that became so massive in one of the pastures that it still defies description. Though if I were to try to describe it, I would start by mentioning that the trunk of the tree at head level is more than eight feet across...

So yes, I still miss it.

But I always find it sad to move. After living in a little apartment in Seattle for a few years, Becky and I moved to Alaska. After the apartment was cleaned out and we were ready to get in the car and drive away, I sat down in a corner against the wall and actually started to feel sad. Not about leaving Seattle, although it is a pretty neat place, but about leaving our little apartment! I guess no matter how unimpressive it was, it was still home.

It is probably a mercy that when we leave our parents' home for college we aren't really moving out, so the actual move is gradual rather than any one moment in time. When Mom and Dad told me they were going to sell the farm, I was depressed and distressed for a while about that. Luckily, it took them ten years to sell it, so the actual event was almost anticlimactic. But it was pretty strange to drive by the farm with Greg, and see different vehicles at the house, the pastures totally overgrazed, and know that I had no real connection to a place that I probably love as much as any place on earth.

At the airport, Greg looked over our fabric-covered antique, which I pre-flighted while Quinn went and started working on contacting Canadian Customs and filing our flight plan. Flight following is required in Canada, and you have to be on a flight plan in America that is handed off when you cross the border, so we had to arrange for flight planning with Seattle Flight Services, which would be handed off to Canadian flight services, and we also had to arrange with Canadian customs for our arrival. We were headed to Kamloops, then on to Prince George. At least that was the intention.

Quinn came back out. "Had to change plans, Kamloops customs agents are off duty today, we would have had to pay a call out fee. So we're going to Kelowna first."

Okay, as I was saying, we were headed to Kelowna, then Prince George. As the sun came up, we took off ("I'm going to glue your hand to the throttle...") and headed north along the Okanogan River. I had been enjoying seeing the country from a new angle, but this was something else again. The sun was barely over the horizon, casting warm amber hues on the sunny side of the slopes and long, deep shadows on the other side. Amazing. The country I grew up in is pretty spectacular anyway, with big rocky hills on each side of the Okanogan Valley ground down by years and glacial activity. Pine trees poke out of the rock crevices sporadically all the way up the slopes, and where the rock gives way to actual soil pine forest dominates.

The strong mark of glacial activity starts with the valley walls, but it is evident elsewhere also. The bedrock on the walls is polished smooth in places where the valley narrows and the ice was squeezed through a tighter spot. Our farm (and the airport as well) lies up on a plateau above the river bottom, in a portion of the valley that was wide and broad. But across the valley to the east we could see the bedrock wall from our house, and in the evening light the rock gleamed like polished stone when we were in our front yard.

Unfortunately, not all of the polished stone was on the far wall of the valley. Glaciers pick up chunks of rock and grind them along in the moving ice. I don't necessarily have much experience elsewhere in the valley, but I can definitely say that the glacier left an extra large helping of these stones behind within the area that my parents eventually purchased for the purpose of teaching young boys to work. Which was at least partially successful…

The down side to having a large supply of glacial stones is that they have to be removed from tilled land (for reasons that are, perhaps, obvious), but there is often not much that can be done with them. Especially with a huge

KOMK to CYLW. Riverside, Washington, in the glacier-carved Okanogan River Valley after departure from Omak just after sunrise.

KOMK to CYLW. Sunrise on the wall of the Okanogan River Valley, with the Cascade Mountains in the distance.

KOMK to CYLW. Highway 97 and the Okanogan River at Tonasket, Washington, where Quinn was born while I was two years old.

volume of them. The rocks are too rounded to make the picturesque walls that are popular in some places. They just make large, jumbled piles of... rock. And digging a hole, for any purpose, was just a trip back through glacial history. My back hurts just thinking about it...

Quinn opened our flight plan while I scanned for aircraft and scenic wonders. Which I was starting to be able to do while maintaining a scan of my instruments as well. Another little bit of progress there, though I continued to struggle throughout the day with maintaining altitude.

I'd finally made peace with the trim system. I had changed the trim so many times by now that I no longer felt that trim was a complication to be concerned about, but rather a helpful simplification of flight duties. We hadn't done a pattern flight since leaving Columbus, but by this point I could no longer imagine trying to fly around the pattern without trimming the aircraft. My, how things change.

But I still hadn't managed to keep my attention on the altimeter as much as I should. In part, I had this sneaking voice in the back of my head, "One of the things that can never help you is the altitude above you..."

When I told Quinn this he acknowledged that it was, "true, but creeping up into airspace used for IFR vectoring by ATC is probably not improving your safety margin."

Right.

Forgot about that.

So on we went, doing less weaving now, but I seemed to be stuck at about 100 feet above target altitude most of the time. And I knew I was going to have to work on that...

Seattle Flight Services opened our flight plan and cleared us to cross the border. After that point we never heard from Seattle again. As we were getting ready to cross we tried to raise them, thinking it might be important to let them know we were leaving their airspace. We got no response. There are an awful lot of mountains around there, so perhaps we were just blocked. Or perhaps they had moved on to more important things and were done with us.

We hadn't been in the air long when Quinn noticed that the time he'd told customs we'd be arriving was going to be way off. He hadn't known how far Kelowna was, as he'd gone in with the intention of filing for Kamloops. Seems he'd been expecting it to be a lot farther than it was. As it stood, we'd be there in a few minutes. This may seem benign, but it is actually rather bad news. Customs is very serious about arriving close to when you tell them you will arrive. That is a challenge in a small plane at any time due to winds, but it seems to be one of their tipoffs for smuggling or some other nefarious behavior. Especially showing up early. And how could we show up early? This plane flies slow no matter what we do?

KOMK to CYLW. Oroville, Washington, out the window as we fly into Canada next to Lake Osoyoos.

"What? Hold on…"

Cancel that. He didn't understand the little GPS unit he was looking at. As it turned out, after we sorted out what time zone and what reporting figure we were looking at, his original estimate was almost perfect. Whew.

I'd read about people having nightmares making the flight into Canada due to failure of the flight plan transition process between American and Canadian flight following. Since we hadn't been able to raise Seattle before entering Canada, we were hoping all had gone smoothly on that end. We had passed along Lake Osoyoos, which straddles the border, then over airports at Osoyoos and Penticton. Both airports had a bit of traffic and the controllers didn't seem alarmed at our presence above their airspace.

Past Penticton, we remained on the west side of the same long, narrow, glacial valley. This was a serious river of ice, we're talking about miles and miles long… As we neared Kelowna, we flew across Okanagan Lake and then over Okanagan Mountain (I've always thought it was funny that the American and Canadian mappers couldn't agree even on how to spell Okanogan/Okanagan), then started descending below a cloud layer ahead of us. We got down to 1,500 feet agl over Okanagan Lake before coming out again into an area with cloudless sky near Kelowna airport, CYLW. The descent set me up nicely for the pattern altitude... but not for the pattern. Mentally, it didn't set me up for the pattern. Right traffic. Ugh.

Now in the textbooks, right traffic always sounded innocuous enough. Why should it matter? You're in the air, flying around, looking at the runway out to the side, but it is on your right instead of your left. So what?

Except I hadn't actually flown any right traffic patterns yet.

Not one.

And to make it even better, the pattern was relatively low over a ridge along the west side of the airport, and as we neared the base leg turn we were looking up at the terrain in front of us, as a high point on the ridge rose into a peak of sorts past the extent of the downwind leg. Double ugh. That pattern flight won't win any prizes, I guarantee it. I felt like everywhere I looked there was something wrong. But we turned based, turned final and found ourselves very high... (I wonder why? Certainly couldn't have anything to do with looking up at terrain while flying downwind... could it...?).

So we employed the Tri-Pacer's famous sink rate to lose altitude quickly and get on the ground safely. Though still not elegantly. I was sure at this point that elegant landings were in my future somewhere, but not, apparently, in Kelowna. I felt like I was starting to figure it out at least a little bit, because I noticed fewer control inputs from Quinn during landing. In fact, by now I was not sure exactly how much he was doing, but I could feel him over there so I thought he was still helping some.

After we taxied to the FBO, we waited while Quinn called customs. Thank goodness his phone worked, mine was completely dead. No Canadian calls for me! They talked for a couple minutes, then decided not to send anyone out to see us, so there we were! Successfully in a foreign country with a little bug smasher of an airplane.

The guys in the FBO were interested in our flight. "Oh, flying to Alaska. We just had a Robinson here flying to Alaska too!" Robinson is a brand of helicopter, but we hadn't seen one... I ordered fuel, while Quinn checked weather to Prince George and filed a flight plan. Then, after the fuel truck finished filling the tanks and I went to pay the fuel bill, my heart stopped. The little receipt had a nice summary of the cost per gallon for Jet A fuel, the number of gallons, and the total cost. Except our plane doesn't take Jet A. Uh oh. I went back to the counter with the bill and pointed out the problem...

"Oh, yeah we actually put 100LL in the plane, that's just an error on the bill."

Right.

Yeah.

So, I went and dipped the tanks.

Then drained a sample and looked it over carefully. It was blue, but that could have just been from the gas that was left over before they filled it.

Since Quinn has actually been around Jet A, I made him look at the sample.

Finally, we hopped back on board, fired it up, and let it run a while. It kept running, and running, so off we went. They really did fill it with 100LL.

We took off to the south, then departed north for Prince George. There is a valley that parallels the Okanagan Lake valley north of Kelowna, and we were asked to stay above the ridge to the east of that valley to allow approaching traffic to have the airspace in the two valleys. So we kept along the ridge and flew up to Vernon before heading north of west toward Kamloops. Quinn was playing with the GPS and trying to get it to make sense to him. He finally realized that the ancient, recreation-user database in the unit wasn't real good for airports in Canada, so then he just put in the Canadian city we were headed for and it worked fine.

A look at our groundspeed and estimated time enroute for Prince George suggested that we should be able to make it comfortably. A pretty long leg for us, but we were flying with a tailwind ("Excuse me! Did you say tailwind? Don't you know we're flying in a Tri-Pacer? Also known as a headwind generator?!?! Didn't you get the memo?") and it was looking good at this point. We altered our heading to the north and off we went, with Quesnel as the fallback in case the tailwind evaporated and took our groundspeed with it.

But it never did. We flew over a patchwork quilt of logging projects, seeing first Kamloops, then a variety of small towns on picturesque lakes slide beneath us. At Missoula and Coeur D'Alene, I had been wondering whether this little airplane had been a foolish venture. And certainly the long flights were exposing some squawks that I would like to have known about before, as Quinn had advised me it would.

But the plane was growing on me, regardless. Maybe that's why when you read articles about Tri-Pacers, the authors seem to have a nostalgic view of them. "If only I still had that little Tri-Pacer..." they seem to say. And yet, for some reason, they are flying Cessna 182s, or Piper Cherokees. If they think Tri-Pacers are really so special, surely they would actually own one? But after thirty hours of flying in one, I confess I was sort of starting to like it myself. A lot. But somehow I think when I am done building time, I might want a bit different plane. We'll see. On the other hand, perhaps I'll never be able to afford another plane, so maybe we won't see...

We sailed right on toward Prince George with our tailwind. We were over mountainous terrain, but not craggy mountains. These were rounded and wooded, and we were flying over a section of high terrain that was almost more like an elevated forest plateau with occasional lakes and a nearly continuous pattern of harvested clearings in the forest below us. The more direct route that we were now taking cut out a lot of distance by not staying along the highway, so we were flying over some country that was accessible via roads but still pretty remote. The lakes that we flew over, tucked in among the hills and surrounded by forest, often had little buildings on them. We couldn't tell whether they were little lodges or private cabins, but they looked like they should have had float planes parked out front to make the perfect backcountry getaway brochure. And I bet that some of them do have little planes parked out front, during the summer...

I worked on keeping my heading constant. We would get a bearing toward Prince George off the GPS, then I would fly and see what direction the aircraft had to point in order to maintain that ground track. Then, I got to try to hold that heading and see how well I did. I tried to identify a horizon reference to help me keep a steady heading. That worked fairly well, but the horizon was fairly unremarkable and there were no peaks in the direction of our travel, so I found that I was constantly reassessing my aiming point.

Inside the cockpit, there are two primary instruments that are used to determine heading. The first is simply a magnetic compass, which looks much like the compass commonly encountered on watercraft. The compass itself could account for all the direction information that was needed if it was a little less sensitive. But the motion of the airplane, in conjunction with the construction of the compass, makes it an unreliable instrument in turbulence or during turning flight. For that reason, a second instrument that is capable of maintaining accurate depiction of heading throughout a steep turn or turbulence is standard equipment in airplanes. This instrument is simply called a heading indicator. Unlike the compass, it will drift off the accurate heading over time, and has to be reset periodically from the compass. Also unlike the compass, it relies on a gyroscope inside of it to keep its orientation, and so it can be used to determine heading throughout a bout of turbulence or during turning maneuvers.

In picking a point outside the cockpit as an aiming point, I would check it against the compass and heading indicator to see whether flight toward that aiming point was leading me to drift from my heading. Periodically, I would have to reset the heading indicator to make sure it matched the compass. Also periodically, the aiming point would draw near enough that the horizon stretched behind it, and I had to establish a new aiming point. This process continued until we were near Prince George.

CYXS. Me standing next to the mighty Tri-Pacer at Prince George, while the deHavilland Beaver behind me relaxes for the winter before it will be put on a trailer and pulled down the runway behind a pickup before taking off and flying away to another summer of work on the water.

As we checked the airport weather update for Prince George Airport, CYXS, the wind on the runway was a slight breeze from the north... but the wind was from the south up where we were. Another long straight-in traffic pattern, but this time with a tailwind. Another new challenge. We got stabilized in our descent, a bit tricky with a tailwind, and then as we dropped below

CYLW to CYXS. Approaching Prince George in the middle of our longest day of flying in the entire adventure.

the trees the tailwind died away and we set right down. Pretty nifty. Tailwind for approach transitioning to a mild breeze from in front at 50' agl. And the landing was almost okay. I've said that so often now that you'd think I could get one right, but after all, I am only flying one landing every couple hundred miles...

We fueled up and Quinn took a picture of me standing next to our cute little bug smasher with a really nice deHavilland Beaver on floats behind me. A couple weeks after the end of the trip, he sent me an email about that airplane.

Seems there was a web video he thought I should watch. Was it the same plane? I cued up the video and sure enough, there it was. It was on a flatbed trailer and was being towed behind a pickup truck out on the runway at Prince George. Behind the airplane was a fire response vehicle (or two? Don't remember...). The pickup truck races down the runway and gets the whole shooting match up to speed, while the pilot in the Beaver rides along until takeoff speed is achieved, then uses the big old radial engine to take off from the trailer, flies over the truck, and out of there! Unbelievable!

It appears that they don't have other landing gear beside the floats, since the aircraft is flown for summer float work only (perhaps one of those little lake developments we flew over coming in?). They land it in the fall on the grass beside the runway, which must have happened not long before we got there on our way through. It seems like you'd want that to be a perfectly greased landing with as little impact as possible...

Somehow they move it off the grass for storage, then put it on the trailer from which it is launched back into the sky with a vehicle assist the following spring. Amazing. I showed the video to a local pilot in King Salmon and he said he had heard of trailers that the airplane just took off from without a truck involved. Apparently having a trailer booking down the runway on its own at 60 mph after the plane lifts off would be a bit of a problem with a nice runway like Prince George's though, since it would likely take out a bunch of the runway lights if it didn't keep moving straight. And let's face it, it's Murphy's Law, it wouldn't keep moving straight.

Another quick turnaround in Prince George, fuel, restroom, preflight, hop in, taxi out, and take off to the north. The slight headwind breeze at the surface that transitioned to a tailwind at 50' agl was a little less entertaining on departure. We reached takeoff speed and lifted off. As we were establishing best climb speed we hit the point where the wind changed, and all of a sudden our airspeed dropped 10 mph. The climb rate dropped a bit, but we were still climbing, and we then quickly re-established best climb. Not a major event, but it certainly got my attention. When there is a shift in wind direction that is known, and it is enough to cause flight safety issues, it is incorporated into forecasts or pilot reports of wind shear. A change of 10 mph doesn't really reach that threshold, but it effectively illustrated for me why a 20 mph wind shear would be important.

We climbed up over the Fraser River, debating what the purpose of the pipeline across the river might be (neither of us had a clue, but then, that's not surprising...), then headed north toward Mackenzie along Highway 97. We weren't actually going to Mackenzie, but that was our initial direction. As we neared MacLeod Lake, we cut across toward the north, crossing the lovely

CYXS to CYXJ. Crossing the Canadian Rockies, the wrong direction, headed toward Fort St. John.

Parsnip (Is that an oxymoron? Lovely parsnip? Botanists and gardeners everywhere are probably offended that I am even asking this question...) River before reconnecting with Highway 97 below us as it headed across the mountains to the east.

The more direct route that people flying to Alaska through Western Canada sometimes take is known as The Trench. It runs north out of Mackenzie to Watson Lake, cutting off a substantial distance involved in flying over to Fort Saint John, up to Fort Nelson, then over to Watson Lake. However, it has a few drawbacks. First, it is too far. We would have an absolute minimum fuel reserve, which would make it technically legal but foolish in 624A. If we encountered weather and had to turn around late in the leg, there would be no alternate airport available within our fuel window, and we'd be well past the point where we could make the return trip to Mackenzie. A one-way trip with no other options. In addition, there is no road beneath. Now we didn't always fly over the road, but it was certainly refreshing to know, while getting familiar with a 57 year old plane, that there was an emergency landing strip available.

Entering the pass we had a massive tailwind (there, I used that word again, unbelievable huh?) and were heading toward rising terrain. We were well above it, but it was a refreshing change to have the updrafts pushing up as we

CYXS to CYXJ. Crossing the Canadian Rockies, the wrong direction, headed toward Fort St. John, sustained by chocolate since we never took time to eat anything else on our longest flying day of the adventure.

CYXS to CYXJ. Crossing the Canadian Rockies, the wrong direction, headed toward Fort St. John, we went over one of the most amazing snow-capped ridges I've ever seen, to the north of us. It was such an amazing sight, we opened the sliding windows to get a better photograph.

CYXS to CYXJ. Did I mention we were flying over the Rockies in the wrong direction? Snow-capped mountains carpet the horizon to the south on the way to Fort St. John.

approached the mountains instead of after we had already crossed them! The sheer lunacy of this leg of the flight was entertaining to contemplate. We had struggled and scratched our way across the Rockies with a fierce headwind in our teeth. Now we were flying back the other way in about an hour total time with a rocketing tailwind helping us out. And having done that, we'd need to fly back across again in future days… if we were going to make it to Alaska.

But no use worrying about that now. Instead, we looked out the window as we crossed over a lake lying at the foot of a massive line of layered rock, set up on its edge, with a light dusting of snow along the ridge. Breathtaking.

On the other side of the highest ridge the earth dropped away, then rose to another slightly lower ridge, a pattern that repeated itself for a number of miles. Approaching each ridge, we would gain altitude as the air rose to cross the ridge, then lose altitude rapidly as the air cascaded down on the other side, carrying us with it. After crossing beyond the mountains, we started a gradual descent to pattern altitude for Fort Peace Regional Airport, CYXJ, at Fort St. John Airport. While we were still twenty miles out, a couple little bush planes took off below us from a field in the middle of nowhere. They flew along at what looked like a couple hundred feet agl, then I lost track of them. A little different kind of flying, that.

We approached the mighty Peace River, quite a sight. (Not sure I've ever heard 'mighty' used as an adjective to describe 'peace' before… but it was a big river…) There was a regional jet coming in, and the pilot thought he'd be to CYXJ after us, but the lady at the airport was concerned that we keep out of the way and repeated a couple times that she wanted to make sure that we were sure we could hold short of runway 29. We were set up for left traffic to runway 20. Quinn stressed the importance of landing where we were supposed to, at the numbers, to give us plenty of room. He had a serious look in his eyes when he said it. As if perhaps he wasn't sure I was up to the task. Seems I'd been leaving plenty of room behind us on occasion…

Buckle up (well, okay, the seatbelt was already buckled, but you can only say tighten your seatbelt so many times…), get sight picture, and then another landing where you might almost think I knew a little bit about flying. Not a lot, but perhaps a little. And we landed near the numbers. We were slowed down to taxi speed more than 1,500 feet before approaching 29. We slowly idled forward from 1,000 feet away, then the lady again requested us to reaffirm our willingness to hold short. Quinn told her that we were planning to hold short, but she then said we could back-taxi to parking if we wanted, as it might be faster.

So… we did. Looking at the clock and the daylight, we had moved pretty fast today and still had a decent window of flight opportunity. So we fueled and headed back out, this time on the way to Fort Nelson, hardly believing that we were going to make it that far.

We had been flying with a tailwind all day, but this time after we took off ("I'm serious about keeping your hand on the throttle and not moving it."— "Well, at least every time I pull it off I immediately recognize it and put it back in a millisecond."—"That is some progress, but I still think we could use some superglue.") it was a crosswind just off our left wing. We flew direct rather than following the highway because we were pushing our time frame and we needed to get down before sunset.

The evening sun was painting the landscape much as the morning sun had done, and we had an amazing view of the Chief River as we passed over. The little pothole lakes up on the plateaus around it had frozen over, it was definitely getting colder here. The landscape was different, a sort of subtle beauty unlike anything we'd passed over to that point. While we were on the east side of the Rockies, and the land was much flatter than what we had been flying through for a number of days, the river valleys carved beautiful canyons with bedrock walls, and the plateaus were high enough to provide beautiful relief in the evening light.

Another more bizarre feature of the landscape that we noticed was the number of lines cleared of vegetation that were all over the place. There were lines that seemed to run north-south and east-west. There were diagonal lines. Each of these lines was a big swath through the woods that went straight for as far as we could see them. They looked like powerline right of ways. Except there were no power lines. And not much evidence of anything that a power-line would run from or to. And there were many, many of these cleared lines. In the middle of really isolated country. Hmmm… I must confess, I still have no clue why they exist. But whatever they are, they show up on Google Maps satellite images.

After another successful landing at Fort Nelson Airport, CYYE, we shut it down for the night and looked for a place to tie down. We were directed to a drain grate near a hangar by the tower personnel, which we tied down to. We then looked around for some hint of the business organization office… this was not anything like the jet-oriented FBOs we'd encountered in most of our stops crossing the United States. There were two hangar buildings. One was the building we had tied the airplane down next to. It was fairly normal except that there was no hint of activity near it. On the other side from our airplane was a pair of single-wide mobile homes with a deck connecting them. And on the other side of these little mobile homes was another hangar that was in the shape and design of a Quonset Hut, a metal building that consisted entirely of a rounded metal roof, with a pair of hangar doors at the front.

I found a gentleman emerging from the Quonset-style hangar and asked about fuel for the plane and a courtesy car. He pointed me toward the pair of mobile homes as the office, and I went in and repeated my request. The gentleman running the show in the office directed me to a courtesy car parked just behind the office area. And what a car it was!

It was enormous. It was a huge red Pontiac from the 1970s that was apparently still functional. Apparently, because they told us to take it. Less apparently, they might have wanted to kill us, perhaps that's why they told us to take it.

While we were getting our courage up for the drive in to town, I called and made arrangements to stay at the local Ramada. We got in the car, and found the remains of a car interior. The cold and the sunlight on the upholstery over 30-plus years had not been kind. Split black vinyl was hanging on in most places. In other areas, the vinyl had long since frayed away, and weathered, yellowing foam was eroding from exposure and use. It was a sorry sight, to be sure. But there was plenty of leg room...

I encouraged Quinn to drive slow, as it was a bit difficult to be certain how icy the roads were. Not to mention how safe this contraption was.

We wandered through Fort Nelson and found the hotel. The proprietor laughed when he saw the car. "Gave you the Cadillac, did they?"

Actually, no, it's a Pontiac... a really huge, thrashed, Pontiac...

The proprietor suggested the Backroads Grill, so we went off in search of it. And in fact, we found it. Unfortunately, he forgot to mention it isn't open Sunday nights. So we ended up having dinner at the famous (?... I'd never heard of it before... but then the local restaurant in King Salmon claims to have world famous potato salad, and I sort of assume if something was famous, the owners wouldn't have to tell you so...) Fort Nelson Hotel.

After gorging ourselves to make up for a day of not eating, I again fell asleep early so I could wake up in the middle of the night and try to find something to occupy me until I could get back to sleep...

CYYE. Killer wheels. No, really. Quinn loved it so much he wanted a photo with the monster car before we handed the keys back in.

DAY 7

*In which we travel a net of zero miles and experience
even more of the exotic flavor of Fort Nelson, B.C.*

In the morning, we dined on the various offerings that made up the continental breakfast available in the office/lobby of the Fort Nelson Ramada. We warmed up the beast (our courtesy car, perhaps we should call it the Red Monster...) so we could almost see past the major frost (uh-oh... frost...) deposit on the windshield, then started slowly creeping through the parking lot toward the road. When we got to the road, Quinn slammed on the brakes and the gas simultaneously and the car lurched forward hard, then stopped.

I found this driving style a bit peculiar, "What was that?"

Actually, he hadn't slammed on the gas, it just felt like it. The brakes were not working... or not working right... Great!

When we got to the airport (without careening off the road, and traveling very carefully to avoid needing to use the brakes), we found... frost. Lots of frost.

I pulled the aircraft up to an attitude that got as much of it as possible oriented toward the rising sun by pushing up under the cowling to extend the nosewheel

CYYE. The FBO at Fort Nelson was primarily these two trailers with associated hangars. The trailer on the right is heated, the trailer on the left has the flight planning room...the very, very cold flight planning room.

strut. I walked around and polished off what I could with my gloves, and then left the airplane to soak up the rays. Except there weren't many to soak up.

Quinn was checking the weather at the little flight planning booth. Which was located in an unheated room. Quinn doesn't like being cold. I'm not saying he didn't do a good job, but I spent a lot of time repeating his flight planning investigations just to make sure he didn't skip on some vital part.

Well, okay, that isn't really true. It is fun to needle him, though. Actually, I knew full well that there was no real circumstance in which Quinn would do anything less than obtain every piece of information relevant to the flight we were planning. But I found throughout the trip that it was difficult to settle in to read anything very thoroughly in the lounge of an FBO when you are waiting to fly. All my mental energy would be on the actual flight, which wasn't happening at that moment. So while I leafed through the magazines, read the occasional article, and listened to passengers, pilots, and FBO employees talking (okay, fine, I 'eavesdropped'), I was almost constantly heading back to the computer to check the flight weather.

The Fort Nelson FBO had an interesting book on the history of the Alaska Highway, which had lots of nice photos in it. That one occupied a little more time than most. But still, I had to go over and check the weather for myself. And boy, it is a lot colder sitting in an unheated room trying to do flight planning than preflighting and polishing off frost in the same temperature out of doors.

Northway was completely socked in. That was, theoretically, our destination. It would have been nearly as far as the Omak to Fort Nelson leg, though, and we were very unlikely to get another day of tailwinds... so we probably were just going to be able to get to Whitehorse.

Especially since the frost was taking its sweet time to go away. Why didn't I get wing covers before this trip?

Frost might seem innocuous enough, but it really isn't. Airplane wings depend on the airflow pattern over their surface to create the lift for flight. The surface texture is an important part of making sure the air flows appropriately, and frost changes this surface texture. Anything that prevents smooth movement of air over the surface of the wings will inhibit the generation of lift, and frost is like turning the smooth surface to a sandpaper surface. It seems minor, but it really isn't.

In addition to the change of texture, ice adds weight. With minor frost, the weight is likely less important than the texture, but other icing conditions can make this a major problem. Encountering freezing precipitation in flight can lead to rapid buildup of ice on the airframe. This changes the flight characteristics of the aircraft both by changing the shape and texture of the surfaces as well as by adding weight rapidly. There isn't any circumstance when ice on an aircraft is a good deal...

Accordingly, the federal rules regarding flight are fairly restrictive where ice is concerned. The only circumstance in which an aircraft can take off with ice adhering to its surfaces is if that ice is frost and it has been polished smooth. Since the definition of polished and smooth are not provided, I take that as license to hang yourself. Better to just get it all off.

As for icing encountered during flight, aircraft that are flying into known icing conditions need to have been approved for that activity. In order to get that approval, they have to have mechanisms for getting rid of ice during flight. This can be in the form of inflatable boots that crack ice off of them (on the leading edge of wings), heat systems that melt it, or deicing fluid reservoirs that weep fluid out onto the surfaces.

Flight into known icing is so far beyond the realm of a little Tri-Pacer that it is hilarious that I'm even mentioning it. But clearing frost off the aircraft is not beyond the realm of 624A, unless we prevent it from ever forming. Wing covers, propeller covers, canopy covers, and cowling covers are all readily available and

CYYE to CYYE. A scenic tour around Fort Nelson while the engine makes strange sounds, but appears to work right. We had intended to go on, but when the engine doesn't sound right, it's time to stop...so we went right back to the airport.

help to make sure an aircraft is protected from weather, ice, and cold. If we had these little implements with us, we would have been in better shape to start up and get out on cold mornings. The wing, propeller, and canopy covers prevent ice from adhering to the aircraft. The cowling cover is actually an insulated blanket that allows the engine to be heated, and that substantially reduces the speed at which engines lose heat. All are wonderful tools for flight preparations in cold conditions. And of course, we had none of them...

Watson Lake was reporting decent VFR conditions with ceilings over 3,000 feet, and Whitehorse sounded a little better than that. Wind wasn't particularly strong in either place.

And the frost was still hard on the wings.

Sigh...

After what seemed like forever, but was actually well before noon, the frost was gone and we loaded up for the next leg of the journey. Quinn filed our flight plan and we got in and fired it up, then waited for the engine to warm up. Why didn't I at least bring an engine heater? Quinn guessed our warm-up time pretty accurately, though, and we were taxiing for takeoff right when we should have been.

We took off and were climbing merrily enough through 500 feet agl when I noticed that the engine didn't sound quite the same. We were flying out toward the west on the north side of Fort Nelson as we gained altitude, and the aircraft had taken on the sound of a helicopter. All engine gauges reported normal indications, but there was an extra "wop-wop-wop" sound. The performance of the aircraft was unchanged. Different power settings corresponded to the same airspeeds as they had previously, but the "wop-wop" sound changed frequency with the engine RPMs.

Having gone through a number of tests, we noticed the cylinder head temperature creeping up. Well, enough of that, we turned back and started descending toward CYYE again. When we arrived back, the controller canceled our flight plan for us, then asked as we were arriving whether we turned back due to weather?

I personally thought that was funny since we had hardly gotten out of sight of the airport, probably about 10 miles out. We told him that we had some indications of an engine issue and wanted to have it looked at. It turned out that a helicopter that had taken off for Watson Lake had turned around due to weather before reaching it, so he was wondering if we ran into a wall of weather. We never got far enough to see whatever weather that was.

When we got back to the FBO we started asking around for aircraft mechanics. The only shop that dealt with fixed wing aircraft (as opposed to rotary wing aircraft, which are usually known as helicopters) was further down the ramp, so Quinn taxied over there while I walked.

As a pre-solo student, I couldn't taxi an aircraft without an instructor, and it is such a process to get us both in the airplane I just generally walked whenever we needed a short taxi. We wandered around through the various helicopter services looking for something that resembled an airplane shop. We came upon an air taxi operator who pointed us in the right direction, toward a hangar that did, in fact, have airplanes parked next to it, and we went in and asked if they could come help us.

"Sure, be with you in a minute!"

We went outside and looked around. Spending time with Quinn at an airport is extremely informative. At Missoula while we watched airplanes all day he had set out to draw the inside of a turbine engine and show me how it worked. And every plane he could spot a corner of he could identify. Uncanny. Of course, he was always like that about cars as a kid, so why should it be any different with planes?

Quinn was always the most technical and mechanical of our siblings. We are two out of a band of four brothers that terrorized our parents and friends around Omak, Washington. In fact, we are the middle two, I'm number two and

CYYE. Waiting for a mechanic...one of the mechanics that worked at the little hangar we took the airplane to was the owner of the little airplane behind me and to my left. He built the airplane himself. I like the huge tall windshield...great for tall people and for seeing over the nose of the plane. The Aviat Husky on my right is a beautiful, new plane, and I'd love to fly floats...but a bit out of my price range.

CYYE. The only hangar we found that had active airplane maintenance going on. All the other shops were working on helicopters. The mechanic's home built airplane looks awfully small, because it is awfully small. But it also looks complete, and functional. The Cessna 206 next to it doesn't look quite so appetizing in its current configuration.

CYYE. The bug-smasher, waiting patiently on the ramp for its doctor visit at Fort Nelson.

CYYE. A deHavilland Beaver on wheels is a pretty impressive looking aircraft, all metal blockiness, but what a backcountry beast. The airplane next to it is the only tandem (one in front and one in back) airplane Cessna made, an L-19. Neither Quinn nor I had ever seen one, but he was sure it had to be a Cessna because of the wings. He was right. As usual.

CYYE. The moment of truth...Quinn didn't know what this aircraft was, but I did...it is a Found Bushhawk. There are a few operating around Alaska, and it is a pretty nice bush plane.

Quinn's number three. Whereas I spent my entire childhood trying to get my work done as soon as possible so I'd have time to read whatever novel I was buried in, Quinn hardly read at all, at least initially. And when he did start reading, he had no time for fiction. Instead, I'd find him reading technical manuals on electricity, or mechanical processes. Of all the people I've known that have taken apart miniature electromagnetic-drive toy cars, only Quinn put them back together as still-functioning toys. And when he started reading Motor Trend he practically knew every make of car and its performance and technical specifications by heart.

So, as you might expect, when he headed to flight school he learned the details regarding almost every aircraft known to man. But here, for the first time, we were getting largely out of the corporate flight environment, and away from airports where the nature of small aircraft transport was primarily travel between one airport and another. Here, in remote northern British Columbia, there were a bunch of bush planes around. The shocking moment of truth came...

"I don't know what that plane is." This was not me talking, but Quinn! Imagine my delight when he was pointing at an aircraft I knew.

"That's a Found Bushhawk." I was very impressed with myself.

We found a tandem Cessna that didn't look familiar to either of us (another one he didn't know!!!) and asked another guy about it (he said it was an L-19, a military trainer made by Cessna). We found a little home built aircraft that had a massive vertical cabin space with a huge windshield, a cute little wooden propeller, and Micro Vortex Generators (VGs) on the top of the wing and the bottom of the horizontal stabilizer. The purpose of VGs is to improve the nature of laminar flow over the surface of the aircraft at low speeds. This makes the control surfaces more effective and lowers the stall speed. Interesting little plane. Turns out it's called a Bushmaster, a common kit plane in rural Canada, according to the owner, who we talked to a bit later.

Finally, realizing that we were freezing, we had been waiting a long time, and we weren't sure what more we were going to learn by inspecting every detail of the deHavilland Beaver, Aviat Husky, and Cessna 185 that had most recently been the subjects of our snooping, I went back to see if the guy had forgotten us.

He had.

I stood inside the hangar and just waited for him to show up. He came bustling around, working on some other plane in the tightly packed hangar. He looked up, got a surprised look on his face, "Oh-Ho! I forgot all about you guys! I'll be right out!"

He came out and we pulled 624A over near his hangar for him to look at it. He raised up the cowling, looked around, then went to the other side.

"Could it be that your exhaust needs to be connected to the number three cylinder?"

I guess it could...

The exhaust manifold that is supposed to be attached to that cylinder... wasn't. When he looked, there was a missing stud. The cylinder head temperature gauge was attached to that cylinder, and the wire ran next to the exhaust connection, which was now blowing straight onto the wire. So, the cylinder itself hadn't overheated, it was just hot exhaust blowing straight onto the sensor. He dug around the shop, found what he needed, and got it all fixed up in a few minutes.

Meanwhile, I was shooting the breeze with the Bushmaster's owner. He was excited about his new Rotax 100 hp engine that he would be installing soon. I have to say, it looked like a really fun airplane. And a massive amount of headroom. As a tall person, I can appreciate that. As a tall person hunched over in a Tri-Pacer, I can really appreciate that.

After 624A was ready, we went back to the FBO and checked weather. But by now it was getting toward 3 PM. Not enough time for Whitehorse in the shortening days. But we could have made it to Watson Lake.

The mechanic who fixed the exhaust had some advice: "You'd much rather be here an extra night than spend a night in Watson Lake... the airport is a long way from town if you get in after people close business."

He also had another now-familiar piece of advice. "When you get home, you should have that exhaust system looked at."

Okay. Check.

The weather for Watson Lake was marginal anyway, so we tied the plane back down and called it quits. We got a room at the Ramada again, asked for a courtesy car, and were pointed to a Volvo. We looked at each other. That car had been sitting there yesterday, too, but we'd been pointed to the Red Monster. Now, the Red Monster was out trying to kill the flight crew from a Citation that was parked nicely out in front of the FBO, and we got the Volvo. Which was, in comparison, almost like a new car. And everything worked! And worked well!

The hotel proprietor chuckled about the car. "Oh, they gave you the nice one this time!"

"Yes, but there's a jet crew driving around here somewhere in the death trap, so keep your eye out..."

Ah, life in Fort Nelson, B.C.

This time when we asked about places to eat the proprietor again mentioned the Backroads Grill. This time, he mentioned that it isn't open Sundays... which would have been more helpful yesterday... which was Sunday...

So we went to the Backroads Grill and gorged ourselves again in the now-familiar pattern of not having anything to eat all day then ingesting a massive dinner.

Ah, flight training...

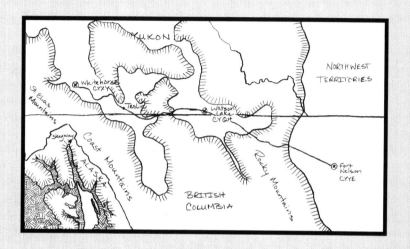

DAY 8

In which we finally depart Fort Nelson
and see many wonderful things and
encounter moderate turbulence
(even Quinn admitted so, after)
on the way to Whitehorse

This day was bound to be different. Things would go well. I was sure of it. Or not...

To start with, surely there would be less frost. After all, yesterday was a bumper crop, it's awful cold here, and hopefully there will be little frost today because it is a pain to deal with and many valuable hours melt away while the frost... doesn't...

With this positive (-ly delusional...) frame of mind, I looked out the window. I didn't see evidence of massive frost layers like yesterday. So far, so good. We got our stuff together and headed down to breakfast again. As we stepped outside we found... frost. But this time the frost wasn't the thick white kind, it was a thin layer on top of solid ice. As if it was a little frost on top of freezing rain. Not what I had in mind.

So much for flying all the way to Northway. The only way we could make it to Northway in a day from here would be for us to get off the ground at sunrise.

We got to the airport before sunrise knowing that we would have ice to deal with. And we did. I went ahead and oriented the airplane for maximum sun exposure and hoped for the best. Then, we hung around and read the same magazines we had memorized the day before. We checked the weather along our route in stages, getting an update on some aspect of the weather, then shuffling across to the warm building where we could let the blood seep back into our extremities before dashing back across to the frozen NavCanada station.

It is fairly important to dress warmly to preflight an aircraft in cold weather. You don't want to rush anything, because you certainly don't want to overlook anything. An added benefit, if you're a bit cold when you get in the airplane, is that you might wear warmer clothes during the flight. Granted, if you pump up the heat inside the cockpit, you might be able to fly comfortably with less clothing.

But I'm good at dwelling on less rosy scenarios. I have a thing about dressing to walk home. That means if I'm in an airplane flying over the mountains, I want to be dressed for walking in the mountains. Just a personal thing. Search and rescue, on average, locates downed aircraft within 70 hours in remote terrain. I'd rather be alive and walking around than frozen to death... because if you are wearing jeans and a T-shirt, and you have to make an emergency landing in zero degree weather, you are going to be facing a serious challenge to live for 70 hours. Flight following can help narrow that time down as well, but that's the basic problem. Always dress for the walk home. It could happen. And dressing for the preflight will help you do that.

But what about dressing for checking weather forecasts in Fort Nelson? Not sure where that helps out. Maybe it helps make sure you dress for preflighting... or even overdress.

Right next to the FBO there was a helicopter, a Robinson R-44, parked. It had covers on the rotors, much like I wished I had on my wings, and a heater rigged up inside. It looked like it was in decent shape to get going at some point. The flight crew was a pair of ladies that came out and started pre-flighting the chopper in mid-morning. We, however, were going to be there a while. I walked out every so often and worked on the elevators and accessible areas of the wings. The ice layer wasn't as thick as I feared, and would break apart if I thumped on the fabric surface. But after discovering that fact, I decided I'd best not run around doing that. I'm not sure what the fabric can take in terms of thumping on it, and decided I didn't want to find out while located in Fort Nelson. That would slow the project down quite a bit... so mostly we just waited.

It turned out there wasn't any real hurry, because Northway weather was limiting flight to IFR again, as it had been for four days. Northway was starting to sound like a pretty limiting location in this schedule. That left us with the possibility of flying to Whitehorse, about half of our original intent in terms of total flight distance, which meant we had plenty of time. Good thing. Watching ice melt ranks right up there with watching paint dry and pots boil (why is it that they say a watched pot never boils, when a pot never boils at all, it is the water that boils…?).

We spent a lot of time getting the rundown on Fort Nelson from the guys in the FBO. The business operations of the FBO seemed to be centered around helicopters, as did most of the other businesses around the field. When I asked about the local economy, I got a snort. Apparently there isn't much of a local economy. So who's paying for all the helicopters? There is clearly some sort of local economy…

The FBO operator seemed to see two pieces of the local economy; timber and oil. He said the closing of mills was hurting the area. And now, in an ironic twist, the dropping of fuel prices after the $147/barrel fuel bubble had burst was hurting the businesses at the airport. Much of the helicopter operations were in support of the various oil exploration activities going on in the region. With reduced oil prices, those activities had been ramped back substantially, and the winter contracts that had been arranged by oil companies had recently been cut in half and might soon get cut further. The profitability of oil exploration was much less when the price of fuel was less.

What about traffic like ourselves?

"The number of people flying the highway over the last decade has dropped so low that it is hardly a blip on the airport activity now. Still quite a few people that drive the highway in the summer, though."

It's funny how different economic challenges can arise from the same circumstances. Here we were in remote B.C., where most people were probably overjoyed at the prospect of more affordable winter heating fuel bills, and yet the FBO was looking at a very severe cutback in their work due to the same root source. At that point, I didn't have a dog in the fight because our fuel prices in King Salmon are set by the last fuel barge, which departs with its load of fuel in September. So I was going to be paying based on $117/barrel prices no matter what the price of oil did over the next six months.

Sigh.

Unlike the previous day, we were actually getting some real sun. The area right next to the hangar adjacent to the little FBO office had pretty decent thermal properties. This was because of the hangar wall reflecting sunlight.

Unfortunately, that was where the helicopter was parked, not our airplane. We were on the other side of the hangar. The R-44 took off well before our little bug-smasher showed any signs of thawing, and with the heaters and covers and sun exposure that was no surprise. I kept checking on the airplane until the ice showed some signs of softening, then borrowed a pail and took some water out there. Very pleasing to watch the problem (that would be the ice, in case you aren't paying attention or my narrative has completely lost you…) go away almost immediately. So finally, after a lovely couple of frosty days at Fort Nelson, we were headed out (again… but this time we meant it…).

The Alaska Highway leaves Fort Nelson to the west northwest, toward Watson Lake. But after a few miles it dips to the southwest into the mountains, in a fairly circuitous route that we weren't sure we wanted to take. At this point in the trip we were faced by a relatively new dilemma. Previously we had been able to fly along and choose which place we wanted to land for fuel at our convenience. Now, we were flying through a stretch of country with no fuel available before Watson Lake.

The distance was not prohibitive, but we were going to be flying west again, which so far had meant headwinds on every leg. Cap that off with the fact that yesterday a helicopter (it is tempting to wonder whether it was the R-44 near us at the FBO, but further thought reminds me that there were a huge number of helicopters at Fort Nelson, so the chances of it being that particular one seem relatively low…) failed to make it to Watson Lake from Fort Nelson and had to turn around. At present, the weather at Watson Lake was good, but there was not a lot of information on conditions in between.

If we were to fly over the highway, we'd always have a landing option for an emergency. But with headwinds, and especially if we had to turn around after getting almost to Watson Lake, we'd be running ourselves short on fuel for making it back to Fort Nelson in case we needed to turn around. As a result, we opted to head straight along the flight path direct toward Liard Hot Springs, then pick up the highway after it swung back our direction. We traded emergency landing surface security for fuel security. Another pilot might have chosen differently, but it is the kind of thing you need to weigh when you are in this sort of landscape. If we landed off-airport, we would be really off-airport.

However, we did have the advantage of flight following, which is a great service provided by NavCanada. The FAA provides it as well within the U.S. It is only as helpful as the pilot makes it, but flight following when properly done can reduce the average time to location of a downed aircraft from 70 hours to less than 24. That's a good thing. Our survival equipment was also a good thing. Two sleeping bags, two sleeping pads (if you've ever been in a sleeping bag on the ground, you might wonder, as I do, why sleeping bags even have insulation on the bottom… it doesn't do any good… you need a pad for that ground insulation even if you don't need it for comfort…), a tent, water filter, an axe, a stash of food, and arctic clothing. All very good things.

CYYE to CYQH. Toad River, running down from the mountains south of us to join the Liard River on the other side of the plane.

So we headed out across the landscape and watched the highway snaking along off to our left before it turned and headed toward the mountains. We had previously flown across an area without access to a highway within gliding distance when we flew from Kelowna to Prince George. After reaching Anchorage, we would be heading out beyond the road system on our way to King Salmon. So in a way it was just part of the gradual transition to backcountry flight. But just because it is going to be part of operations when we get there doesn't mean that a safety valve should be discarded lightly when it is, in fact, available.

We set our heading and I held it pretty well for a change, toward Liard River. About halfway to the river from Fort Nelson, we flew up over a set of cliffs as the land rose beneath us. The cliffs folded back and forth on either side of us and then faded off into the distance on either side. The strange lines cut into the treescape were still there below us. In fact, they are so prominent that after the flight I looked up online aerial imagery of the region and they show up clearly. I also tried to look up some hint of why they are there, but so far have not found any explanation. Weird. We flew on and reached the confluence of the Liard River and a tributary flowing into it from the south, the Toad River.

In Alaska, we have very few amphibians (biologically speaking, lots of amphibian aircraft...), and the only one out in King Salmon is the wood frog. In fact, I've only seen one wood frog the entire time I've been there, which was captured by my kids. They wanted to keep it, but we couldn't find anything it would eat, so we turned it back loose... We do have another pet frog from a pet store in an aquarium in the house though... so I guess I didn't quite tell the truth about there being only one amphibian out our way...

I wonder how the Toad River got its name? Biology, or a personal insult to somebody?

As we reached it, the land below us gave way to steep cliffs again, and the valley dropped away on either side. The confluence of the rivers was a fantastic sight, not only the joining of two waters but the joining of two canyons with different formations. Somehow as we approached, and the cliff wall dropped away beneath us, we failed to notice that the lines across the landscape had disappeared. We had too much to look at to think about them. Whatever inspired people to cut lines into the forest, it didn't inspire them to do it in steep areas. We never saw the lines again.

The Liard River was a beautiful and magnificent sight. The rock walls along either side were pretty impressive, and we flew above the water for a while as the river wound through the Grand Canyon of the Liard. Usually when they name something a 'grand canyon' it is an indication of some sort of scenic, well, grandness. This one certainly didn't disappoint. I'm a bit of a river junky, so I was trying to add in to my visual scan a segment where I would look down to identify rapids. Well, as would continue to be an issue, it is hard to see things at 3,500 feet above the ground. I could see whitewater down there, but the actual features of the rapids were impossible to guess at that height. Probably a pretty impressive place from down in the river, that's for sure. But I didn't then and still don't intend to find that out while flying this airplane...

While I was looking for rapids, and other airplanes, and checking the instruments (see how hard I was working?) Quinn got distracted by some lovely lakes to the north of the river, which I never even noticed until looking through photos later. We flew over the Egnell Lakes a few miles later on, but when I went back to match the photos Quinn had from the trip, there were a couple that

CYYE to CYQH. We flew so fast the camera must have been shaking... but there we are...I look like I've lost my razor...if you can see me through the blur...

CYYE to CYQH. Canadian Rockies along the Liard River.

didn't make sense with any of the lakes on the map...so I went onto Google Maps and surfed around the satellite views until I found the lakes from the photos. There they were, along the Grand Canyon of the Liard. I totally missed the lakes, too much to see. I guess I'll have to go back... how disappointing.

Our arrival over the Liard River also confirmed that we had returned to mountain flying as

CYYE to CYQH. The northern side of the river had gentler terrain.

we sought to cross the Rockies, again... We were once again entering into a valley, flying along with peaks above us on either side. We passed over Liard Hot Springs, where the Alaska Highway came back to meet our flight path, and then headed upriver. The nature of the mountains gradually rounded, then opened back up into a larger basin as we approached the settlement of Coal River.

As we flew along, we could see a line of black ugliness ahead of us and above. Hmm...

Black ugliness is not my favorite.

We had a good view ahead of us for many miles out, and could see that the direct path, again leaving the highway (but this time as the road wound north), would take us under the least ominous looking clouds. And in fact, as we got closer it looked as though we had the best spot, as the ceiling above us was higher than on either side, so we didn't have to lose precious altitude. We scooted under the line of clouds as we crossed over some small lakes, the Egnell Lakes, and peered ahead to notice another, though less dense, line of clouds ahead. This one was lower, so we dropped down to get under it as we crossed another major river, which was unnamed on our chart and on every other map I've come up with since then (only in the uninhabited reaches of the world can a body of water that large be without a name on a map…), then maintained 2,000 feet above the ground instead of the 3,000 we had been enjoying.

We got the automated weather for Watson Lake, then dialed in the frequency for the airport and listened for a while. It's always good to listen before barging in on a radio frequency. For one thing, the radio transmissions can't be understood when more than one person is talking at once. For another, if you listen you might learn important things, and get a sense of what things you need to convey when you enter the conversation. Much of the time we had been monitoring radio frequencies just to help us maintain situational awareness of other aircraft. This time, we heard… nothing.

When we reached 10 miles out we advised anybody that was listening that we were coming in to land at Watson Lake Airport, CYQH, then went back to listening. We had been working our way into a headwind all day, and now at the very end of the journey we were to have a tailwind, though slight at only 5 knots.

Another plane reported that they were coming in from the northwest to Watson Lake. It has a nice long runway, so when I asked about flying the pattern to land on runway 8, Quinn suggested that we just fly straight in for 26. Well, okay. I like the straight-in part, but landing with a tailwind is a new trick. Not the sort of thing you do when you are dealing with a short runway, but in this case we had 5,500 feet and even with me landing we are usually getting down and stopped in less than 3,000. The plane is capable of a lot less, and hopefully I will be too…

For once, I was not feeling behind the airplane. Being forced to descend a bit to get under clouds earlier had kept me from being as behind as I seemed to be prone to putting myself, and now I was enjoying a nice long look straight down the runway. I ran through my checklist, changed power and pitch to set us up at approach speed, and monitored the sight picture out the windshield as we sailed in for landing. It went… well. Not a 'greaser' by any means, but it was without question a fully competent landing that felt okay.

I was a little bit in shock. After all my crummy landings, there was a decent one! Maybe I can do this after all! I danced a mental jig, while taxiing off the runway. I don't know if Quinn noted the improvement as much as I did, he never said. But he was probably relieved. It was the first landing I made where I didn't spend the next hours quizzing him over what had gone wrong, or how I needed to change it.

The facilities at Watson Lake are reminders of a past that is fading away. There wasn't always an Alaska Highway on which you could drive to Alaska from points south and east. Most early transport to Alaska was by ship. At the beginning of World War II, the Northwest Staging Route, a set of airfields through Canada to Alaska, was identified by the Canadian government, and select runways were lengthened. The U.S. used this string of airports to transport aircraft and supplies to Alaska and on to Asia (mostly to Russia).

The Alaska Highway followed later, and came about as an attempt to improve the access provided by this air route by allowing surface transport. Watson Lake was one of the airfields expanded as part of these efforts, and as we pulled up to fuel the airplane, the hangar looked like it might have been from that same era. The huge, multi-paned glass windows letting in light high up on the walls of the wooden hangar definitely invoke a feeling of a time gone by. Modern hangars seem to be almost completely constructed of sheet metal. Windows are the exception rather than the rule. Of course the metal hangar can be relatively well insulated, which is good in cold northern summers. But it is completely black inside without extensive lighting, and an entire day working inside a hangar like that seems almost like… well… an entire night working in a hangar like that. Modern progress.

We were pulled up outside the hangar next to the semi-self-serve station. It was mostly self serve, but the guy running the FBO at the cool-looking hangar came out to start the pump and we had to go to his office to pay. I didn't look at the price of gas, I was scared to. I figured it likely beat even King Salmon prices for heart-attack potential.

Right behind us at the pump was the Cessna 172 that had arrived after us. They had come from Whitehorse, where we were heading, and had a semi-encouraging report to go with the semi-self-serve station. They said that we should have no problems if we followed the highway. They, on the other hand, had come through the mountains to the north of the highway and ran into problems in the form of clouds. I didn't get the specifics on how they dealt with that, but we were planning on following the highway anyway, so off we went.

Like many of the places we landed at, we never saw anything but the airport other than from the air. I'm not sure how much we missed at Watson Lake, but one of the major attractions that I've heard of, if it can be called a major attraction, is a signpost forest. Apparently, the original signpost forest. Calling it a forest implies that the signposts grow there… which I don't believe… But

CYQH to CYXY. Along the highway out of Watson Lake, next to the Rancheria River, was a little clearing. Perhaps somebody wanted a private landing strip, but that's probably just the one-track pilot mind. Likely had nothing to do with aviation. Didn't see an airplane or any obvious sign it was an airstrip... but it should be...

CYQH to CYXY. As we flew into the pass on the way to Teslin Lake, Veronica Lake was south of the highway ahead of us and the road snaked ahead, our long emergency runway, leading us all the way to Whitehorse.

people apparently have collected all sorts of signs and put them up on posts, and there are a bazillion of them there. I have no idea whether I would like it or not … since we didn't go and check it out, but in the realm of random and crazy tourist attractions, this must rank up there with the odd ones.

The breeze was still light, so we took off on runway 26 and climbed out toward the mountains. As we labored to gain altitude, which seemed to be the normal situation for 624A, we headed west.

Watson Lake is in a rather broad valley, and we were crossing it to reach the mountains again on our way to Whitehorse. Behind us, to the southwest, the route known as The Trench led to (or from) Mackenzie, and another VFR route took off to the south into the mountains. But our route was along the Alaska Highway. The airfield at Watson Lake is rather north of the highway, and when we took off we were traveling a bit north of west. We swung around to the west, but after flying for five or ten minutes we didn't have the highway in sight and Quinn was looking around at the ground features and finally decided it wasn't worth risking missing the highway to try to fly direct, so we turned a bit more south to make sure we intercepted the road.

Just after turning toward the south, we finally crossed a spur road and spotted the highway. Of all the places the highway could be routed into the mountains, the correct valley wasn't easily identified from the air until we had the highway beneath us. When we reached the mountains, we were flying at an altitude of 6,500 feet mean sea level and were level with the tops on either side of the valley. The highway stretched beneath us, a ribbon of road, offering a welcome token of security.

At this point, I told Quinn that since we were flying over a river, he should keep his eyes peeled for critters on the sand bars since visibility is good there and our chances of picking out an animal are higher. Bears are the primary river walkers out where I live, so I was thinking about seeing bears along the river. Or maybe moose. So he looked. And looked. In fact, he looked off and on for the rest of the trip, but never did see anything. Then again, flying more than 3,000 feet above ground level, that isn't that surprising. A little eye exercise …

We emerged into the valley of Teslin Lake a few miles on. Bristol Bay, Alaska, which is the region where King Salmon is located, is filled with large lakes. Naknek Lake, right up the river from us, is the largest lake that is completely within a national park, and it is big. To get to King Salmon from Anchorage, we fly over Iliamna Lake, which is even bigger. Huge. Basically an inland sea.

I'm not sure how big Teslin Lake is, but after flying through the mountains, it looked mighty impressive, a huge long ribbon of a lake stretching out in either direction before us. We crossed over the village of Teslin and the runway there and headed on up the lake.

The structures below us that made up the community of Teslin looked much like the bush areas of Alaska. The houses were set in among trees and surrounded by four seasons worth of construction materials, blue tarps, and vehicles. The order of suburban America was far behind us now, and homeowners associations weren't controlling the lawn care or decoration of property. Everything looked utilitarian around the buildings, accentuated by the lack of foliage on deciduous vegetation and the dirt roads.

The color of the water was a steely gray-blue, the gray likely coming as a result of the reflection of the clouds above us. The wind, which had been whipping all day up at our altitude, was moving pretty good on the water as well, and the entire lake was a sea of white caps. As we neared the northwest end of the lake, the water changed color to a beautiful shade of a lighter, richer blue as the lake got shallower and we could see the bottom. Teslin Lake is basically the upper end of the Yukon drainage (though technically, the Teslin River flows into the Yukon as a tributary, and the headwaters of the Yukon River proper are slightly to the west).

I wonder how many salmon swim this far... it is an amazing journey. Salmon in Bristol Bay don't have much river to buck to reach home, usually less than 100 miles. By comparison, salmon must pass more than 1,000 miles up the Yukon River just to reach Canada... and they they still have a long way to go to reach Teslin Lake.

Salmon reproduce in freshwaters at high latitudes, where there is relatively little productivity in the lakes and rivers. This means comparatively little predation compared to the very productive northern oceans, so the young salmon that are born have less chance of being eaten right away.

But these unproductive waters aren't so good if you're a fish trying to grow very big. After a couple years of getting slightly bigger, they go to the ocean and spend a couple years there, becoming much larger very quickly. But to complete the cycle, they have to swim back up the river to breed. Salmon swimming up the Naknek River by our house have all of 30 miles to swim from the ocean before reaching Naknek Lake. The really long migrations around Bristol Bay might be more than 100 miles, though not that much more. And we have a lot of salmon. Teslin Lake is more than 1,000 miles up the Yukon River drainage. It looks like a great salmon system, but I bet it has a lot fewer salmon than anything I'm used to... if it has any...

Biology aside, it is a lovely place. The narrowness of the lake, combined with its great length (around 70 miles), is fairly awesome. With the slight angles in the lake basin, it appears to stretch off forever as it disappears around a bend in the valley up ahead. We stayed along the highway until we reached the lovely blue shallow end.

As we reached the end of the lake, we turned southwest to fly along a valley that led over toward Whitehorse. We had descended to 5,000 feet to maintain cloud clearance, and were in a rather narrow valley, though with plenty of room to turn if need be. The winds in the valley were rather fierce, but relatively smooth, until we finally reached the far end. All of a sudden we went into roller-coaster mode and my head hit the headliner. Wow. I'm not one of those loose seatbelt kind of guys. Seatbelts only work if they are properly located and snug, and mine was snug. But I still hit the headliner. Wow. Quinn kept looking straight ahead, unperturbed as usual. Okay, nothing special going on over here, I'm just trying to keep my head down and fly the airplane. The turbulence continued for a couple miles as we emerged from the pass, then abated as we turned northwest toward the upper end of Marsh Lake.

We called Whitehorse approach as we neared the end of Marsh Lake, and they requested that we report again when we crossed the dam. The dam. Where are we going to find a dam?

We peered over the map, then finally found it on the river (not just any river, the Yukon River…) and started looking for it. We found the real one, not just the one on the map, sliding below us and contacted ATC again. They directed us to land on 13L (when there are parallel runways with the same magnetic direction, the L refers to the one on the left and the R to the one on the right… 13L would be the same pavement as 31R, and 13R would be the same stretch of pavement as 31L). As we entered left traffic for 13L, Quinn told me that the Canadian traffic pattern is to fly the entire descent straight in, which means that the downwind leg needs to be extended. The downwind for left traffic to 13L was taking us right over Whitehorse. We turned in and I followed up my fabulous (okay, maybe that's a stretch, but it felt fabulous to me…) landing at Watson Lake with a not-so-fabulous landing at Erik Nielsen Whitehorse International Airport, CYXY. Got behind the plane on descent, then sort of muscled it into landing. Not. So. Fabulous.

During the period where I was training for ground school, I kept reading descriptions of flight where people were, "getting behind the airplane." It seemed odd to me, I couldn't really understand what they were talking about. But when you drive a car, you have to do things in a certain order to make things work smoothly. For example, if you are pulling up to an intersection where you are going to make a 90-degree left turn across traffic, you have to be scanning for oncoming traffic, reducing your speed to a safe turning speed while maintaining a consciousness of the traffic crawling up your bumper behind you (and moving over to get out of their way, if possible), putting on your turn signal to warn people of oncoming traffic, shifting down if necessary, and executing a turn when you reach the proper location with safe conditions. Many of these things are second nature.

But imagine that you were overwhelmed by some of these responsibilities, and forgot to slow down. Now you have a vehicle moving at a rate of speed that is too high to execute the turn comfortably. You may even be in a situation where the vehicle is moving too fast to execute the turn safely. You are behind the vehicle.

With aircraft, the biggest problem (in my somewhat limited experience) was basically the same as that in vehicles; slowing down. I needed to gradually reduce the speed of the airplane as I entered the traffic pattern and landing phases, and stabilize at the speed that would allow me to do the maneuvers slowly. But there is no brake on the vehicle (at least, not one that works while flying), so all speed control is done by changes in application of aircraft attitude (or pitch) and power settings. It is the same principle, but it takes longer to make it all work, so you have to start earlier. I wasn't doing so well at that on many of these approaches. I definitely needed some practice in the traffic pattern.

The American traffic pattern, with the descent for landing starting when the aircraft is flying downwind, away from the runway, requires two turns during the descent. The Canadian pattern, with the extended downwind leg followed by a straight-in descent, requires no turns during descent. So it really should be easier to fly, it is much closer to the straight-in landings I was growing so fond of. But I still got behind the airplane.

Still.

Got.

Behind.

Practice needed…

But there we were in Whitehorse, Robert Service country, almost on the marge of Lake LeBarge (actually LaBerge… but apparently that didn't rhyme as well…).

Robert Service was a poet that wrote about the Yukon, primarily the gold rush in the Yukon. One of his most well-known poems, The Cremation of Sam McGee, takes place on, "the marge of Lake LeBarge." Which, as I was now learning, is not how it is spelled. But hey, he was a poet. While the pilot license I'm hoping to earn will be awarded based on my ability to do things in a certain manner and follow rules, poetic license seems to refer to breaking any and all rules. Apparently, including spelling. And I guess, technically, I'm exaggerating as well, since Lake LaBerge is twenty miles north of the Whitehorse airport, so we weren't quite on the 'marge' of it yet.

We unloaded the plane and headed into the FBO to evaluate our options.

The FBO was nearly deserted, so I looked around in the pilot's lounge at the advertisements for lodging. While we were there, I found a gentleman in one of the (apparently) leased offices and he recommended the Airport Chalet, so we decided to head over and get a room.

Before we left, a couple aircraft arrived. One was a Cessna 172. In fact, it looked like the same one that landed after us in Watson Lake. And a crew came in from an R-44 that had landed out of sight on the field. Turns out they were flying the chopper to Alaska and had been making roughly the same trip we were. They had come through customs in Kelowna the same day we did (just before us, based on the comments from the folks in the FBO), but then were delayed while a maintenance issue was sorted out. They were thinking about heading on out, but there were icing conditions at Haines Junction, so they ended up at the Airport Chalet as well.

There were rooms for sleeping in the FBO itself, which would also have been fine, but I had no Canadian cash and wasn't sure how I was to arrange payment, since there wasn't anybody staffing the FBO. The Airport Chalet sort of reminded me of the days of Robert Service, 1890s to be precise, though I don't think it is that old ... quite ...

The interior is dark wood paneling. Our first year and a half in King Salmon we lived in a place with a dark wood interior. I'm a firm believer in white paint. Interior walls in the north should be bright for winter cheeriness. After living in a dungeon for two winters I feel qualified to have that opinion. I suppose yellow would be passable. But dark wood is definitely not my favorite interior. Dark, dark, dark.

The restaurant was again the high point since we hadn't eaten since breakfast, so we went and gorged ourselves. The walls of the hotel and restaurant are covered with photographs of airplanes of all shapes and sizes, including a couple really nice shots of Twin Otters flying low over mountain ridges. That is an impressive looking plane. I had a long time to look at the photos, because I was so hungry the minutes seemed like hours while we waited for the food.

I guess the food must have been okay, because I don't remember it ...

DAY 9

In which we eat three meals, consider flying
to Skagway, and generally do nothing

Wednesday dawned slow and cold. As usual on this trip, I woke up before dawn. As we traveled north, and dawn arrived later, that was becoming less and less of a challenge…

Northway had been IFR for days so we were not really expecting (though we were certainly hopeful) that it would be a lot better. We went out to the front desk of the Airport Chalet and found that there was a computer that could be accessed by coin meter, so we went ahead and exchanged some cash for Canadian currency, then checked the aviation weather. There was only one computer available, so we took turns spending money at the little meter while the other entertained himself. While Quinn was on the computer, I wandered up and down the long hallway to our room and beyond, looking at the photographs hanging in the rather dark corridor (… did I mention how I feel about dark wood paneling … ?). A number of the photographs were of historic Whitehorse, almost all of them somehow related to the airport. Many airplanes. I squinted in the dark to see them. Okay, I'm exaggerating. But it was a dark hallway.

Weather at Northway was below VFR minimums. Hmm… We ate breakfast and checked again. After all, checking weather is a pilot pastime and a lot can happen in an hour. Right?

Still IFR.

We checked with the front desk and coaxed them into letting us extend our checkout time to noon instead of eleven.

We headed over to the FBO and I went out and checked the airplane. I tightened the tie-downs, checked the oil, and went back in. On my way in, I stopped and admired a beautiful Maule M7 sitting outside the FBO. I rode in a Maule once, an M5. Maules are the closest living ancestor of the immediate predecessor to the Tri-Pacer design of 624A. They are made with tube and fabric, except that the wings have been changed to a sheet metal construction. Bedford D. Maule's experience building aircraft, so the rumor goes, was from working on the PA-20 (the tailwheel Pacer that preceded the Tri-Pacer) as a Piper employee. Then, he went off and designed his own aircraft based on the Pacer. Subsequent years have seen a number of changes to the Maule design, but it is specifically designed for backcountry work, primarily to take-off and land in as short a distance as possible (short take-off and landing, or STOL), and it has four seats (newer designs can be configured for six).

When I got into that Maule M5 a few years ago, I sat in the back seat, all 6'4" of me, and fit. Clearly they've made some changes, as I definitely wouldn't fit in the back seat of 624A. I made a mental note to check the Maule out later if it was still there. After arranging for the plane to be fueled I bought some Shell 15W/50 aircraft engine oil and went out to top off the little eggbeater engine on our craft.

On my way, I grabbed Quinn from the pilot lounge and told him to come and ogle the Maule with me. We looked it over pretty good. It had wing covers on, which I envied since my recent frost encounters. The aircraft was either nearly new, or superbly maintained, or both. Beautiful big Alaska Bushwheels, an interior that seemed from a distance like it would be small but appeared very large when we peered in the windshield, with a lovely panel and upholstery.

Hmm…

Maybe someday…

Bushwheels are made specifically to improve take-off and landing safety and performance on rough terrain. They are huge, as large as 35 inches tall, and are made with soft rubber. With only partial inflation, they are like big, floppy, shock absorbers that roll. The modern video classic on the utility of these huge tires is Greg Miller's Big Rocks and Long Props. I'm not really interested in the kind of tight situations they put themselves into in that video, but Greg flies a home built version of a Maule on huge Bushwheels, and it's pretty amazing stuff. I'd settle just for the Maule.

On our way back to the hotel to make a final decision on whether to stay or go, we passed the R-44 crew headed to the airport. They had checked out and were going to the official weather briefing station before launching. Helicopter pilots have a different set of minimums, and a lot more options when confronted with declining visibility, so they were thinking that the weather might allow them to make Northway. The pilot was pointing out to us that he could get shut down by low clouds, and just land in any clearing. Quinn shook his head as we walked away.

"I know what they are saying, but after years of weather flying it just seems wrong to say that you'll put yourself out in that kind of situation and then just set down and wait it out. That doesn't work with an airplane, and it's hard to imagine changing gears to take that approach even if it does work."

We went ahead and checked the weather at Northway ourselves, found it was still IFR, and verified with the hotel that we would be staying another night with them, then consoled ourselves by eating lunch in the café and looking at the photos in there.

More airplanes.

More photos of the airport.

As we finished, the R-44 crew was returning and checking back in. It turned out that there was a strong icing system in the Haines Junction area. The different minimums for helicopters don't apply to flight into known icing conditions, which is not something they could mess with, so they were back as well.

We admired the airport windsock out the restaurant window. Whitehorse has a really fabulous windsock. Technically, I guess it should be called a wind indicator, because it is most definitely not a sock. It is actually an airplane mounted on a pylon that weather vanes to face into the wind. In fact, the airplane is a DC-3, a bush freight hauler from bygone years. Despite the antiquity of the design, they are still in service, and there is one that flies cargo to King Salmon on a regular basis. Quinn said it was the coolest windsock he'd ever seen.

After an arduous afternoon of watching TV, we ate dinner, watched some more TV, and looked at maps. Whitehorse is not really a long way from Northway, but we had a weather front in the way that was challenging. Whitehorse is also not far from Skagway, which had good VFR weather and everywhere in between was flyable.

I had really hoped to avoid coastal southeast Alaska. I've never been there, so perhaps I shouldn't have such an aversion, but it seems to be full of foul

CYXY. Quinn wanted a photo with the coolest windsock ever. This DC-3 is mounted on a pylon, and turns to face into the wind, so it really does function as a wind indicator. A really, really big wind indicator. Very cool.

weather. But Quinn had two weeks leave for this trip, which was eroding quickly. Our time window wasn't going to last forever. It was Wednesday at this point, and Quinn was due to fly home from Anchorage on Saturday. When Quinn left, I would have to find another pilot to help me get the plane home, and that might take me a while and a bunch of logistics. I really needed to make sure we got the airplane to Alaska, if possible, before we ran out of weather and time. I felt like the process for international flight was not too scary, but leaving the airplane in Canada and coming back in who knows how many months didn't sound like it was going to be quite so straightforward.

I went back out and put some more Loonies in the computer and checked the Skagway forecast. Hmm... Sure, it was good weather right then and the following day, but a huge mass of ugliness was sitting in the Gulf of Alaska and moving in over southeast Alaska, and winds in excess of 60 mph were due in the next couple days. Scratch that.

Northway looked like the only option, and maybe I'd just have to hold Quinn into his workweek. Oh well. His wife lives too far away to kill me easily. It would be nice if she would let him visit again someday though...

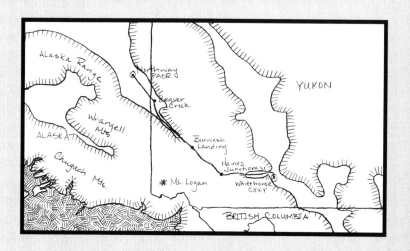

DAY 10

*In which we depart Whitehorse for Northway
and spend a long time with the customs office
while weather arrives and traps us there*

Thursday morning we checked the weather and it was decent. Not great, but VFR at both Whitehorse and Northway, and all reporting points in between. We ate quickly and got ourselves over to the airport. Quinn got on the phone for a briefing and to file our flight plan while I preflighted the airplane.

The preflight inspection is a funny thing. In theory, it isn't really any different than getting ready to drive a car in the sense that it is a good idea to check out all the things that could go wrong before you get in the vehicle and get moving. When the earth was young and I was in high school taking a driver education class, they taught us the importance of checking the car before getting in and getting going. But nobody does pre-drive inspections on a routine basis, and the habit is never really established.

Many, though certainly not all, potential consequences of a poorly performed pre-drive inspection are relatively benign though. Some exceptions would be brake failure at a bad moment or a wheel coming off. But if the engine quits we limp to the side of the road and stop. Ditto with parts and pieces falling off, like hubcaps and bumpers. And if the muffler comes off, we drive by all our friends' houses and through various neighborhoods, revving the engine extra loud… or maybe that's just some of the people I know…

The consequences of a poor preflight inspection are a bit more alarming to contemplate. It was no accident that the first thing Quinn had shown me, a day before we even flew the aircraft, was the preflight inspection. When something goes wrong in an aircraft, limping to the side of the road has a very serious vertical component to it. A number of the parts and pieces that might fall off could make it impossible, or virtually impossible, to land in control of the aircraft.

If you have the experience and creativeness of Barry Schiff (a well-known pilot and author) you might be able to land an airplane using the doors to turn (he has really done this, as a demonstration). But for the most part, if ailerons or rudders come off, or control cables break so you can't use them, there is a serious issue. If a wing falls off, well, let's not think about that. Instead, let's just learn to do a proper preflight inspection. Because of the seriousness of the situation, the preflight is a heavily emphasized part of flight training, and it is fully ritualized into a habit in the first part of that training.

The inspection includes every moving part and every surface on the exterior of the aircraft, the engine oil and gas system, the electrical system, flight controls, and engine function. It is performed in stages, and is done with a checklist. Most checklists are just what the manufacturer recommends. For a plane as old as 624A, the operating handbook didn't include checklists. We had a checklist that the former owner put together, and we went through it in detail back in Columbus, making sure it included everything it should.

After we had a satisfactory version, we printed it up and had it laminated, and this was what guided our preflight inspections. It had served us well so far, though we discovered that one of the routines was still missing a fairly important item. It turns out that you do have to turn on the magnetos in order to start the engine, no matter how warm the engine is, even though that wasn't on the checklist for a hot start…

It was cool, but the wind overnight both the last two nights had prevented any frost from forming on the aircraft, so we didn't have to spend time dealing with that. The weather briefing was for visual flight conditions all the way to Northway, but with some potential for marginal conditions to be developing over Haines Junction, which was where the icing was the day before.

We got in and fired it up and waited a bit for the engine to warm up. The R-44 crew had headed off to their ship while we were getting information on weather, and said they'd race us to Northway. Some race. We figured we'd give them the head start so NavCanada would be able to report back if there were any weather problems. Or… maybe we were just slower to get ready…

We were cleared for takeoff on 13R, and as soon as we got off the ground the climb rate dropped. It wasn't quitting on us, like our heart-stopping experience back at KVTA, but we rotated for takeoff, got 100 feet up, and then the climb rate dropped to only around 200 feet per minute. While 624A is not going to win any climb records, we were usually getting 500 feet per minute. The engine was running fine, the aircraft was in the proper climb attitude, and we were at the best rate of climb speed… so what was happening?

The weather system that was arriving was bringing wind over the mountains, and we were cleared for a right turn as we departed with the goal of flying in the direction that was behind us. So we were going to be turning a full 180 degrees, basically flying the crosswind and base segments of the traffic pattern, then leaving straight. But we were taking off from 13R, which put us in a right traffic pattern. The first right turn onto the crosswind leg pointed us toward the mountains and the wind. The downdraft that came over the mountain was pushing on us, holding us down while we climbed through the falling air.

"We're not climbing very well…"

"It's okay, we're still climbing and our speed is good, just maintain the pattern while you climb."

We made the turn to downwind and were still barely gaining altitude as we traveled along the upwind side of the airport. Surface winds were low but generally from 150, so the choice of takeoff runway made sense, but the rather poor climb ability of the Tri-Pacer in conjunction with a downdraft left an unsettled feeling for a few minutes as we headed up along the mountains in full climb the whole way. A little north of town we were going to be turning west with the highway again, and as we turned into that valley we ran into some pretty good turbulence again.

Funny, ten days before when we ran into turbulence I kept waiting for the wings to fall off. Now I'd just sit there trying to maintain course and let the airplane ride the bumps. Sometimes the plane tilted up on its side and sat there for a moment too long, and I would try to level the wings. But for the most part I found that responding to the bumps does no good and just raised my anxiety. I wouldn't want to ride with an anxious pilot, so I'd started focusing on just letting the airplane ride the air, which was not always smooth…

The continued downdraft was getting a bit nerve wracking though.

"I'm going to move out into the center of this valley to see if we can get away from this downdraft over here."

Quinn sat silent, looking out the windshield, though he did turn and smirk at me when I looked over for some confirmation of my stated intent. Since he didn't say not to, I ventured out farther away from the hillside and all of a sudden we were in an updraft. All the altitude we weren't gaining due to downdrafts was now delivered to us rapidly. I love updrafts. Quinn was probably smirking wondering what took me so long…

A few miles later, as we flew over the Dezadeash River ("The What River?"— "Don't worry, I've never heard of it either…"), we could see the ceiling lowering ahead. All that altitude we rode up on the updraft… we gave up as we rode back down to make sure we stayed below the cloud ceiling.

We were approaching Haines Junction, the site of the icing conditions yesterday. Quinn was looking at the maps, and he said that the location of the weather front coming over the mountains made this the spot along our route with the most likelihood of having clouds spilling down. Which was easy to say, since he was, at that moment, watching the clouds spilling down…

Of course, the wisdom of his statement could be tested by seeing whether the weather improved on the other side of Haines Junction. We descended to 1,000 agl and started continually judging the visibility ahead. Amazing how short even five miles looks. The visibility continued to degrade until I felt as if we could barely see as we neared Haines Junction.

Flying in those conditions, after hundreds of miles of flight with visibility in excess of 40 miles, is startlingly claustrophobic under visual flight rules. With moderate snow cover, white sky, and flat lighting, it was especially noteworthy. The time and opportunity to see other traffic seems really limited with that combination of factors. But at this point, we'd already passed my comfort zone (that happened a few times, as you'll perhaps recall) and were flying on Quinn's expertise and his comfort level. In fact, we passed out of my comfort zone about ten miles before Haines Junction.

But Quinn helped me to get a sense for the distance by continually pointing out the distance ahead of us. Anything less than ten miles felt like poor visibility to me, but as we neared Haines Junction we could see the runway out ahead of us.

"How long do you think that runway is?"

"I don't know. Why?"

"Because it is 5,000 feet long, which makes it basically a mile. So how far do you think we can see?"

"Oh… well then, probably three miles."

Yet it felt like terrible visibility. As we turned northwest out of Haines Junction, I was hoping for an immediate improvement in visibility, but it wasn't there. The conditions stayed the same as we flew along. I found myself trying to climb again, much as I had the first few days of the trip, by instinct and not need. Quinn would push forward on the yoke until I was back at 1,000 agl, saying that, "visibility is better here, we need to see as well as we can."

Okay. But he had to do that three or four times. A little dose of tension in my arms and a climb is virtually guaranteed.

There is a little pass northwest of Haines Junction on the map. It is slightly removed from the highway, which passes west of it. We opted to fly the highway all the way, in part because we were ensuring our escape route. We could turn away from the highway in the direction of the pass, which would allow us to descend during the turn while maintaining the ground clearance we wanted, as the ground would be sloping down.

"We have plenty of space and visibility to turn around, so relax and just maintain altitude and monitor the conditions to make sure they aren't deteriorating."

They weren't deteriorating.

It's just that I wanted them to improve, that's all…

The road ran up over a ridge just east of the marked pass, which was actually just the lowest spot on the ridge (actually, it wasn't much of a ridge, really just a high spot that marked a drainage divide) that crossed the valley. On the other side of the divide, we could see Kloo Lake off to our right, then another smaller lake just next to the highway. The visibility might have been starting to improve, but neither of us dared to mention it at that point.

Then, as we were nearing Silver City, the visibility abruptly improved and we were able to see for miles out ahead of us again. That was definitely more to my liking.

It turns out it was more to Quinn's liking as well… he allowed as how that little section was… let's say… suboptimal…

Actually, what he said had something to do with the reproductive apparatus of small equines…

"That sucked donkey balls!"

?!?!

Donkey balls????

?!?!

That's strong language for Quinn, a bit shocking actually.

"What did you say?"

"I said that sucked donkey balls!"

I stared at him, a bit incredulous at his language.

"Well, it did!"

…so I guess he wasn't quite as comfortable with it as he had made out.

Flight into poor visibility conditions that then become worse may be the most popular (not in a good sense...) way that pilots rated only for VFR flight find themselves flying solely by reference to instruments. According to legend (which may be true, but I have been unable to verify it...) floating around on internet forums, a flight school used simulators to examine the survival time of VFR pilots in instrument conditions, and it was amazingly terrible. Without training in flight solely by reference to instruments, most pilots couldn't survive five minutes after entering clouds. Spatial disorientation, which started soon after entry into the clouds, resulted in the pilots ending up with the aircraft upside down and spinning out of the clouds to the ground. Sometimes they were totally unaware of the situation right up to impact. Whatever the details of that study might have been, VFR flight into instrument flight conditions is one of the top killers of pilots.

The current training model requires every student pilot to fly for a minimum of three hours solely by reference to instruments in order to qualify for a private pilot license. The goal is to make sure a pilot can at least execute a 180-degree turn back the way they came, in order to escape the conditions. But by far the best way to avoid these situations is to make that turn while you can still see...

Students don't take their instructors and bust into a cloud bank to practice flight in this manner. Instead, they put a shield over their eyes that lets them see only the instruments ahead of them, and the instructor maintains visual separation from other aircraft while instructing the student what to do. The instructor also places the aircraft in unusual climb and descent attitudes and then asks the student to recover the aircraft. In terms of training, all those flight still lay ahead of me. For now, I was just tickled to see miles and miles ahead of us...

Quinn is a very experienced instrument pilot. But that didn't mean he could just take 624A into the clouds and be fine. The instruments that allow safe operation in clouds are not all present in 624A. Further, the instrument routes that are assigned by air traffic control in mountainous areas are at higher altitudes in order to keep the aircraft safely above the tops of mountains along whatever route is being flown. Our climb-challenged aircraft would not easily transition to the needed altitudes for instrument flight in the mountainous area we were in, even if it had been equipped with the proper instruments. We were fortunate that we were able to fly through in VFR conditions. Our only alternatives would have been to stop or turn around. Judging from the "donkey balls" comment, it appeared that we nearly did turn around...

At Silver City the highway jogged southwest around Kluane Lake before heading northwest again. I was turning southwest to follow the highway, but Quinn looked at me quizzically...

"Where are you going? Go across there."

"I don't like open water…"

Well, I am a fish biologist after all, and I love water. But not in an airplane without floats. We were regaining altitude now that conditions allowed, but I just couldn't help but look at that water with a healthy dose of fear.

If I have on a drysuit and appropriate layers underneath, I'll swim in almost anything. Lacking that, I was really not interested in any scenario that had the potential to put me in the water. We likely would never have been beyond gliding distance of shore or Quinn wouldn't have suggest the straight route, but I didn't have the gliding ratio completely wired into my head yet.

"How about if I fly along the shelf of ice." The shelf I was referring to had formed over the southern end of the lake and at least would give us something to crawl out on. It seems odd that I am so interested in flying and yet I manage to think of all sorts of worst possible scenarios for every situation.

I've run the glide ratio numbers in my head a number of times since the trip. The best glide speed is 90 mph with a descent of a bit less than 1,000 feet per minute. This is roughly equivalent to a loss of slightly under 700 feet per mile (of course, I'm not accounting for added effects of wind …). So we needed 3,500 feet to make the five mile distance across the lake at a glide, and actually we needed less because we could have turned toward the shortest distance to shore, which might have been behind us. With proper knowledge, I should be able to recognize distances better than I currently do from the air, and that will help me make decisions like this one with the appropriate information instead of just my native caution. We may have been high enough by that point, but I hadn't done the math then …

Along Kluane Lake we encountered some broken, low clouds beneath us, but they cleared up again after a few minutes. Near the other end of Kluane Lake we broadcast notice on the airport frequency at Burwash Landing that we would be flying over. They had a message for us from NavCanada to contact the flight following frequency. It turned out that they were talking with Northway about our arrival time, as there had been a snowstorm in Northway and they were concerned about whether they could get the runway plowed in time for us to land. That sounded serious!

We told them our estimated arrival time to Northway, and they told us they'd update us later. Maybe we'd be in Burwash Landing for a while waiting? In the meantime we continued on past Burwash and headed along a fantastic valley.

The spruce forest was dotted with tundra and ponds below, with slightly rounded hills on either side of us. Ahead there was a cloud layer at 2,000 agl that was thin and gauzy, and we decided to look at it from above rather than descend down initially. That turned out to be a good choice, as it was so thin we could see through it, in addition to being patchy, so we were now flying above a wispy layer, below a layer much higher up, in between two sets of hills and with more hills visible beyond the near ones.

Surreal.

Clouds have got to be one of the best (…and worst…) aspects of flying. The wispy layer faded away as we neared Beaver Creek, the last landing option in Canada before crossing the border. NavCanada contacted us again, told us that the Northway field would be ready for us, and cleared us to cross the border. And oh, by the way, they've cleared the ski strip, not the main runway, at Northway.

Huh?

Out came the Alaska Supplement, the little book that is reprinted every few weeks that gives all relevant information available for each airport in the state. In the contiguous 48 states, there are Airport/Facilities Directories (AFDs) published that provide all the relevant information for each airport. There are a bunch of different regions, each covered by its own AFD. Alaska doesn't seem to rate an actual AFD, we only get a supplement. But it seems to work.

We'd been flying with the equivalent publication from Canada, which has the entire nation in it and is three inches thick, but it was now time to downsize. The Alaska Supplement probably barely makes an inch. It has some interesting material, though, like the arrival and departure procedures in Skagway… maybe it's good we didn't go there… looks a bit tight… they don't even have room for the traffic pattern…

Northway has a 6,000 foot runway, but it was damaged in an earthquake and still hasn't been fixed after a few years… weird. The portion of it that is still in service is approximately 3,000 feet, but wasn't apparently a high priority, because they weren't plowing it. Also weird. Adjacent to the runway is a taxiway that has been expanded into a ski strip for winter and a gravel strip for summer. It is 2,000 feet long. By now, I had landed in less than 2,000 feet. But I hadn't been required to. And I hadn't landed on something as narrow as this little strip coming up.

Beaver Creek was, like many small towns along the route, not much of a town. We looked at the runway there. Runways are almost always wider and straighter than the road, but the Alaska Highway is a pretty nice looking ribbon of hope below a small craft. After passing over Beaver Creek, we sailed on a few miles up the road, but hadn't gone far when I spotted the border.

"Okay, we're crossing the border right now."

"Yeah? How can you tell?" Quinn was challenging my position finding abilities, looking out the window and seeking some telltale landmarks by which

I might be able to make such a definitive declaration. There were some cabins, but my assurance had nothing to do with them.

"I can see it. The border. Look, it's right there." It was dead obvious, though Quinn was a bit skeptical while I was pointing it out. He still had his nose buried in the map and wanted to know how I was so sure. But there, out the window, another line like those that surrounded Fort Nelson extended off into the distance through the spruce trees. Somebody, somewhere, cleared the entire border for miles. Cross-referencing to the map verified that it was, indeed the border. Once again… weird. But weird or not, there we were, entering Alaska and leaving behind Canada after flying through some fascinating and beautiful country.

The trip from there to Northway was fairly anticlimactic. We had good visibility, we knew they were waiting for us, and we flew along over frozen tundra woodlands with the highway visible off to our right.

As we neared Northway, an airplane came on the radio and announced his departure from Northway. He took off and headed out, and after we picked him up among the trees and bogs covered with snow, it helped us to identify the airport. Northway is not on the main highway, and the runway is oriented perpendicular to the direction we were traveling. As a result, it was not as easy to pick up visually, but we found it, then set up left traffic for runway 7L, the little ski strip.

The approach presented an odd sight picture, as the huge opening is all around the main runway, while the strip is right along the end next to the trees. As we turned final, Quinn got a look at how small and tight it was and invited himself to do the landing.

"I'm going to do this landing. My airplane."

"Your airplane."

Probably a wise move. It really did seem small after all the landings I'd been doing on huge, paved runways. Amazing to think of all the flights bush pilots make onto gravel bars and the like, and I'm struggling to get the sight picture for a 2,000 foot ski strip. Quinn, however, cruised into 7L at Northway Airport, PAOR, as if it was the simplest thing on earth. Which, for him, it probably was.

We taxied up toward the few little buildings, near where the R-44 was parked (yep, they beat us…) and sat and waited in the plane. A few minutes later the R-44 crew walked by on the way to their helicopter and waved, and right after them came a Chevy Blazer with official-looking emblems on the side. Customs.

They came over, asked a few questions, looked at a few of our bags, then invited us to come in and fill out some paperwork. There was an older gentleman training a younger gentleman on how to do the work. Apparently, there is a customs station at Tok, where they are usually stationed when they are not at the airport. But in the time when the ports of entry were set up, Northway was

PAOR. Looking down the hall in the Northway Lodge, a one-of-a-kind place.

the airport designated, and not Tok. This is a bit odd now, as it isn't entirely clear that Northway would exist in any real fashion other than the airport, which is really not much of an airport...

This was the young man's first day at the airport. He seemed very sharp. However, the older gentleman was too busy shooting the breeze with us to be much help, so the process took a bit longer than it might have. This was, in no small part, our own fault, because we like talking to people. By this point in the trip, we specifically liked talking to people besides each other. We had done plenty of brother to brother chattering over the previous days, and expected to have plenty of time to do it some more. And as it turned out, we were going to have plenty of time to talk to people in Northway in general, because we spent so long in customs that when we left the office to head back to the plane the weather was looking unfriendly. Oops.

We filled up the tanks and called to check weather. Not good. Not only was the weather getting marginal where we were, but it was getting even worse in the passes. Between us and Anchorage lay a huge wall of nastiness. And Northway was IFR. So we ordered lunch and asked about a place to stay.

At this point, it is probably appropriate to admit that of all the places I've been Northway has got to be one of the most hilarious. The place you go to ask for gas is the Northway Lodge. Actually, the kitchen of the Northway Lodge.

They also have a bunch of quarts of 15W/50 aircraft oil sitting in the kitchen that you can buy. The dining area is the entrance, and connects onto what appears to be a bar that wasn't in use. Connecting back between the bar and the kitchen is a hallway that has rooms on either side.

"Yeah, we were wondering whether there is anyplace to stay, in case we can't fly out today?"

The man I was speaking to looked a bit worried, "Yeah, we have some rooms back here. And, well, we did just have some people staying last night, you know, and they left this morning, but the maid just quit today, so I'm not sure when we can get a room ready."

Okay, so they could probably get a room ready, but it might be a little while. Good to have options if the weather stayed down. I wasn't too worried about the maid problem. I've been known to make a bed when the situation is desperate enough…

We ordered lunch and waited to see the weather improve. Watching for weather to improve… watching paint dry… watching pots boil… highly profitable and entertaining activities…

After we ordered, a stream of people arrived. It turns out that the local village elders had arranged to eat there at the same time we did. Which was fine, except that it took over an hour to get our food. Good thing we're pilots (okay, he's a pilot, I'm a student, but I'm starting to feel like one). We hardly eat all day anyway, so we're used to hunger.

Seriously, I have a very twisted view on the food habits of aviators after this trip. Or maybe they really are as deranged in their eating schedule as we were?

After the mad rush on the diner was over and we had finished lunch, we called for a weather briefing again. Conditions were still IFR in Northway, and even worse in the mountains between us and Anchorage. You might wonder how it could be IFR right where we were, without us being able to tell?

The area around Northway is pretty flat, so we didn't have a great way to determine horizontal visibility unless it was greater than about seven miles. The height of a ceiling is equally hard to judge in a flat area. Around mountains, you look at a map, figure out what contour line you are seeing up to, and it gives you a decent idea. We couldn't tell if the ceiling was at 200 feet or 2,000. But the little automated weather device at the field claimed it knew what the ceiling was, and it claimed it was pretty low. Since the clouds were a solid, dark mass above us, we took its word for it…

So, we abandoned any plans to leave and asked them to get that room ready.

The man got a worried look on his face and reiterated, "Okay, I think we can find somebody to help get a room ready, but it might be a while."

"Well, we're not in any great hurry. And if you can get sheets and towels delivered, that is all we need. We won't be going anywhere…"

We still had a lot of time before evening, but we knew we were going to be here. We also started asking about where to tie the plane down. A lady named Marcy, who had just entered, shared some local frustrations.

The state of Alaska had designated an area near the end of the taxiway as the place for tie-downs, but had not provided any electricity there. The only place where there was electrical service was off of a house that one of the locals residents lived in next to the lodge. So if we parked where we were supposed to, we wouldn't have heat for the aircraft. And if we parked where we had heat, we wouldn't be able to tie it down. I was then asked to write a letter to the state expressing my frustration. Actually, probably expressing her frustration.

I hadn't been there long enough to get frustrated yet. And, as a matter of fact, I didn't have a heater, so what would I plug in? When I asked this question, the man turned to another man that was walking through.

"Hey, do you know where that heater is that we used to help that guy get his plane started last month?"

Last month… not a good sign. They were pretty sure they had a heater somewhere, but it was such a vague answer that I assumed not. We parked the airplane at the tiedowns and lugged our gear back in time to choose a room, which hadn't been cleaned.

After we watched a couple TV shows, somebody came with sheets and towels and we were good to go. Dinner followed, and we watched the temperature gauge outside the window, which had been reading around 10 degrees F during the day, drop toward zero. Hmmm. Going to be cold all right.

In the afternoon, we had listened to one of the employees complaining to Marcy about his coworker. Very entertaining in a sort of people-watching way. Normally in an airport you get to see lots of people, but we really had a good time watching people here. Because there were few of them, so we got all sorts of detailed insights. During dinner, the shifts had changed, and the coworker was there. She also sat down and spent a good while complaining to Marcy about the gentleman who had been complaining about her.

Fascinating. They were both great to us.

Having had all the fun we could stand, we headed for bed and called it a day.

PAOR. Home sweet lodge room, in the one and only Northway Lodge.

DAY 11

In which we preflight the airplane but are unable to start it, which leaves us stuck in Northway and prevents us from ending up stuck in Fairbanks

Friday dawned very cold. As in -7F. That's a minus sign in front of the 7, in case you missed it. We called for a weather briefing, and the weather, well, it stunk. We were stuck in IFR, but with a slight ray of hope in the forecast for later, but all the passes to Anchorage were forecast to be socked all day.

So, we ate breakfast. Important, they say. Breakfast helps start your day off right. Or something like that. We asked about checkout times, as we didn't know when we'd be leaving (but then, in a little airplane, you never do know…).

The response was a bit confusing… "Well, I don't know when we'll be able to get the rooms cleaned if we can't find somebody to work."

I found that confusing, anyway. I wasn't sure how I'd be affected by the business' ability to get the rooms cleaned.

Nevertheless, we preflighted the aircraft, which was again blessedly free from frost (thanks, most likely, to a good wind all night), and kept working the phone for weather briefings. The weather in the mountains between us and

Anchorage continued to be terrible, with low ceilings, mountain obstruction, and turbulence. The forecast picture in that direction was not changing, so we finally gave up on getting to Anchorage.

But if we did come up with a plan, the aircraft was ready!

I had to get to Anchorage at some point, because it is the logical departure point to get out to King Salmon. But at this point I was more directly concerned with getting Quinn to an airport where he could fly home. The following day, he had a scheduled departure from Anchorage International Airport to fly home to Columbus. My goals for the day had shifted to the point that I was now hoping that we could fly somewhere that would allow us to get Quinn into the realm of scheduled air service. Preferably in time to hop on an aircraft that was heading to Anchorage to meet his flight. Quinn's wife had been taking care of their six-month-old son for almost two weeks, and he was under no uncertain understanding that he was supposed to be on the scheduled flight home.

But there is no scheduled or unscheduled passenger service from Northway, at least not in October. A gentleman that flies for the US Fish and Wildlife Service came in for breakfast, and he came over and talked to us to find out what in the world we were doing in a Tri-Pacer in Northway (okay, he didn't really ask that, but I figure most anybody that encountered us was probably wondering that in addition to what they were willing to actually ask …). We chatted a bit and told him about getting stuck here yesterday when the weather shut down on us.

"Too bad you couldn't get to Tok yesterday, it's a real town," he said.

Yeah, too bad. Salt in the wound.

Another gentleman at breakfast turned out to be the person responsible for plowing. He seemed like a fine guy, but we realized after listening for a while that he didn't exactly relish plowing all the time for little or no aircraft traffic. And he didn't seem to have a consistent plan for how to do the plowing. They had a bit of a roundtable discussion among the locals that morning about the different ways he could plow. Pretty funny, really. We were just glad he was, in fact, plowing.

Fairbanks weather was flyable, but Northway was IFR for the entire morning. Of course, the only reason we were looking at Fairbanks as an option was that it was a place with a heavily used commercial airport. But in October, flying toward Fairbanks (really cold) when you want to be flying toward Anchorage (merely cold, not really cold) is just sick and wrong. Desperate times call for desperate measures.

Around noon, weather at Northway started looking suspiciously hopeful, so we ate lunch and were peering out the dining area windows when we observed blue sky peering through the clouds. In a few minutes, a huge section of sky had cleared around us, though things still looked black and ugly toward Anchorage.

But at least we could get to Fairbanks. I called for a briefing, and the weather continued to be decent in Fairbanks (except the temperature... but that was pretty poor where we were as well...) but the briefer seemed a bit agitated that we were thinking of taking off. She was, "still showing IFR conditions in Northway!"

I thanked her, then went and loaded the plane. What can you say to that? Visibility unlimited except toward Anchorage, sky unlimited, not sure how to respond to that being classified as IFR. We preflighted the airplane again, since it had been sitting a while, and got in.

And it wouldn't start.

The battery was pretty sluggish anyway, and we weren't getting any firing at all, and after a few tries the battery was truly dead.

Those lovely magnetos that make an aircraft operable without electricity also make it possible to start an aircraft such as ours when the battery is dead. BUT (pay attention...) this means the person pulling the propeller through its rotation is standing out near the propeller when the engine fires up! VERY DANGEROUS IF NOT DONE CAREFULLY!

So, we discussed safe techniques for hand propping, what each of our responsibilities were, and then Quinn got out to try it. Nothing. He started panting and looking tired.

"Do you want to trade and let me try a bit?"

"Go ahead..."

I took a turn. Nothing. I started panting and looking tired. It isn't that easy to do.

"We've probably iced the plugs, because it isn't even trying to fire, so we may as well stop."

In between gasps, I agreed, but asked, "What does icing the plugs mean?"

"Some water vapor is drawn into the engine with the fuel. If it freezes on the spark plug contacts, it prevents the creation of a spark. It's impossible to start and engine after that without melting the ice off. At this point, we aren't going to be able to get the aircraft started unless we can heat the engine."

How are we going to do that? I wasn't feeling quite so nonchalant about the electricity/heat/tiedown location issue now. Maybe I should write the state a letter about the facilities at Northway after all. Probably after I obtain a heater... We tugged the airplane up the taxiway to the house that had an outlet available. The manual labor taxi effort warmed us up greatly, though I suspect it didn't do much for the plane. I can't say for certain, as we didn't try to start it again. Then we asked for a heater, and they set about trying to round one up.

And the hours ticked away.

And further away.

Pretty soon it was obvious that we weren't leaving Northway that day, as we were running short on daylight. I went back and asked about a room, and again got a bit of a runaround involving housekeeping.

"We really don't need anything cleaned in the room if we are going back to the same room with the same sheets and towels."

"Oh. Okay, here are the keys."

We slogged our stuff back in and moved back in for the night.

My next task was to work out a plan. I now knew that we were not going to be getting Quinn anywhere that night. Which was Friday. He was due to leave Anchorage the following evening, which was Saturday. I considered renting a car for Quinn, but I didn't really see any cars available at Northway for rent. Among the crazy ideas that came to mind was rounding up somebody to drive out to Northway from Anchorage, which would allow Quinn to drive back… but it is a very long drive…

I decided to start calling people I knew to see if they could assist with this plan or come up with another one. I also decided to start by calling my pilot friends, since I would also need somebody to come meet me and help me get the airplane back to Anchorage. Someday I'd be qualified to fly it myself, but that time hadn't arrived.

My friend Chris, from Naknek, was the first person I called with this foolish grasp at nonexistent straws, and he turned out to be unavailable at the time but a helpful voice of reason.

I tried out my best wild harebrained idea on him, asking him whether he could get to Anchorage on the evening commuter flight and drive out. It's hilarious in retrospect. That's a long all night all day no time to waste kind of an assignment, and who wants to take that on at short notice?

Chris shrugged off that idea like the offal it was.

"Get that battery out of the aircraft and get it on a charger in a warm place. Do whatever it takes to find a heater to get some heat on your engine. You need to get the battery and the engine ready to start above all else, or weather won't matter. And don't fly further north under any circumstances."

Right. Check.

Back to work harassing people about a heater. I like to think I'm a kind and gentle person, which prevented me from expressing my frustration at the time. Let me just say now that I'm glad I didn't explode.

We finally rounded up a tarp and a little portable space heater. It would have to do. I spent an hour or so trying to figure out how I could make a little cocoon around the front of the aircraft and make it airtight. The heater was too large to put under the cowling anywhere, so it pretty much had to sit on the ground. The tarp was draped over the prop and around the nosewheel, and double-wrapped to help seal it. I borrowed pieces of wood and rocks laying nearby to seal the tarp against the runway. The room heater sat next to the nose gear and chugged away. That evening I went out and found it was 53F in the cocoon. I turned the heater down to maintain 43F and hoped it could keep up overnight.

In the evening, the forecast had turned completely hopeful for Anchorage, so we abandoned the rather hopeless task of finding another alternative way to get Quinn to Anchorage and focused on making sure the airplane was flyable so we could get there in 624A.

We also rounded up the use of a battery charger and put the battery on a plastic bag on the floor in our room, charging happily in the corner. On one of my trips out to check on the heater, I found it had fallen over and shut off. It then took me a good 20 minutes laying out there on the tarmac to get it back on and revise the tarp to make sure it wouldn't tip over again. Or at least, I hoped it wouldn't tip over again… morning would tell that story…

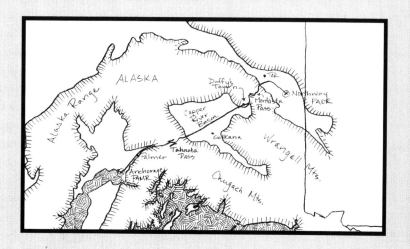

DAY 12

*In which we fly to Anchorage with glorious
weather, at which point Quinn deserts me even
before we check weather for the final leg*

Saturday dawned gloriously clear and bright. We dressed extremely warmly, settled our tab, which now included electrical use (If this seems petty, you have no idea how expensive electricity is in bush Alaska. Most electricity is generated by diesel power, and fuel prices were just starting to come down from the immense peak from earlier in July. Furthermore, the price of diesel was compounded because the transportation of diesel to the remote locations required extensive movement over road or air or water or some combination. So believe me, I wasn't complaining about paying for the heat and battery charging.), and headed out to the plane.

This time, we installed the battery, took off the shroud, noted that the temperature was only 35F (but that was better than the -7F outside), and started it right up with no problem. We let it warm up a bit while we listened to the automated weather report and evaluated our options.

The ski strip is 2,000 feet long, and that's all that was open. The orientation of the runway is 07L-25R, which means we could either take off flying east or west, and we had an east wind at 7 mph. Ordinarily, that would clearly mean take off to the east. However, there are trees at the end of runway 07L, while the end of runway 25R provides a very long open area cleared for the main runway.

Quinn opted to take charge of this takeoff, "I think I'm going to be doing this takeoff, it's a bit tight..." and he felt better about the open space ahead with a tailwind than trying to clear trees with a bit of a wind assist. Especially since those very trees would block the wind as we reached that end of the runway. Of course, this also meant that he didn't have opportunity to threaten me with the old 'glue the hand to the throttle' trick.

We taxied down to the end and turned, then he put in power and as we neared flap speed he put in one notch of flaps. A moment later, as he was preparing to put in the second notch, the plane lifted off, and the second notch of flaps dropped the nose even as the plane lifted up, which felt almost like a little elevator.

I've felt that a number of times riding in float planes, but didn't realize what I was feeling. But the full-flap trim gives a noticeably nose-down pitch even in climb. Another tidbit of information, filed away. And of course, as befits a Tri-Pacer, we found that the tailwind on takeoff was quickly converted to a headwind in flight. Which is as it should be.

So we were in the air and we headed toward Tok, where we intended to follow the Glenn Highway through the mountains to the Copper River Basin. By now, between Montana, Idaho, Washington, British Columbia, and Yukon Territory, we'd seen an awful lot of mountains and passes. But they just don't stop being gorgeous. Every one has its own special flavor.

We were now in the coldest weather of the trip, and the snow cover was better than we'd seen so far, which enhanced the visual impact of this segment particularly. In addition, the pass was relatively narrow, with fairly rugged rock walls, draped with sheets of snow. We wound our way along, looking at the map, watching for traffic, monitoring the instruments, keeping an eye on the road below, and enjoying spectacular rock walls below and beside us. The steepness of the walls was unnerving, it made it seem even narrower than it, in fact, was.

Following along, we popped through the narrowest gorge of the trip, a little unnamed (at least on the sectional) pass to the south just before Mentasta Pass. We emerged with the highway at Slana and Duffy's Tavern. Both places were new to me. As were Northway and Tok.

After sixteen summers in Alaska, and living here continuously for over ten years, I've still seen very little of the state. That's not surprising. It's huge. Working and living out in Bristol Bay, I've seen quite a bit of neat country that few people would get to match. But all in southwest Alaska. My experiences in

PAOR to PAMR. We had a nice wind overnight, which kept the frost off the airplane, but these two fools (wait, am I talking about me?) got in the airplane and closed the windows while the engine warmed up...I've since learned that if you want to do that you need to open the side windows and freeze a bit...but it's worth it because that way your breath doesn't freeze on the windows.

PAOR to PAMR. A view of the mountains near Mentasta Pass.

the rest of Alaska amount to quite a bit of time in Anchorage for business, and short visits to Seward, Homer, and Fairbanks.

So our Alaska voyage was going to be new country for me until we reached Palmer, just north of Anchorage. I'd heard of all these places, though. Now, I even know where they are. With the exception of Northway, which I saw perhaps a bit too much of, the others are familiar only in general geographic terms, since I only flew over. But it was still wonderful to get a chance to see parts of the state that I had only heard of.

At Duffy's Tavern, the huge Copper River Basin opened before us. I'd heard people talk about going to the Copper River Basin. I'd even looked at where the Copper River was on a map a few times. But the basin itself completely overwhelmed me. It is a vast, open flatland surrounded by magnificent mountains, especially the mountains of the largest National Park of them all, Wrangell St. Elias National Park. Wow.

We got a bearing from studying the sectional, and headed across the vast basin. I assigned Quinn moose patrol duties (well, okay, technically I couldn't assign him anything, but still it makes me feel powerful to claim I did...), but the consistent problem of altitude reared its head. Oh well. I really like 3,000 feet above the ground, and if the airplane seemed to like 8,000 feet I'd probably like that. At this point, we were flying at 4,500 feet msl, and Quinn didn't find any moose.

I, on the other hand, didn't find any aircraft on the horizon anywhere, any deviation from our 117 mph airspeed, any deviation from our heading of 210, any deviation from a wings-level attitude, any vertical movement (starting to get this holding altitude thing down a bit), any anomalies in the cylinder head temperature, or any indications that our fuel burn was anything other than expected. All of which I considered to be good news.

And although we didn't find any moose, we did see some little cabins on Crosswind Lake off in the distance to the north of us, as well as a hint of Gulkana to the southeast. We crossed over what looked like a dirt road in the middle of nowhere, but might have been just an ATV trail that was overly wide.

We met up with the highway again as we neared Tazlina, with Tazlina Lake visible off to the south. From there we headed for Tahneta Pass, a feature I'd never heard of, and Sheep Mountain, which I had heard of, and which lies next to the pass. Along the way, we passed cabins off the highway that had their own little dirt strips, which looked mighty short. Super Cub strips can be astoundingly short compared to what 624A requires. Especially compared to what 624A requires with me at the controls. As we neared Tahneta Pass, we had our first good look at a glacier for Quinn, off to the south of the highway.

PAOR to PAMR. Tahneta Pass out the windshield, a glacier coming down from the left.

Sheep Mountain turned out to be a fairly impressive little chunk of rock, rising up steeply in the middle of a low pass, like a forgotten mountain stranded by creation of a valley that accidentally got split in two. We crossed Tahneta Pass and followed the highway around to the south of the mountain. On the other side of the pass, the terrain of the valley bottom was especially impressive. First we flew past the Matanuska glacier in what was probably our closest glacier view of the trip. Then, the river bottom downstream of the glacier was a massive, wide bed strewn with boulders and cobbles where glacial runoff events kept the flood-plain scoured. Rugged looking country, and steep rock faces on either side. If I had to guess, I'd put many of those boulders at sizes similar to my house.

As we turned south we could see the Palmer Airport beckoning. We notified local traffic, then passed over it at 4,500 feet. But we could see up ahead that we were going to have to drop down a bit. Around Eklutna, the clouds were well below us, but with clear area beneath, so we started a descent to 2,500 feet. Meanwhile, Quinn was studying the Terminal Area Chart for Anchorage, and especially the restricted area southwest of Birchwood.

"Okay, you see this area over here, that's restricted area and we need to stay on the east side of the highway to avoid it." We had not heard anything about its activity when we got our flight briefing, and it's better to be cautious.

As we forged ahead, moving along near the highway, we called Anchorage approach control. We were given an altitude of 2,000 feet, but around Eagle River it started snowing on us and we had only marginal visibility to the ground. We requested 1,000 feet, which was authorized, so we immediately descended to that altitude which improved the visibility despite the continuing snow for the next few miles. We flew on to Anchorage at that altitude. The visibility improved significantly in the few minutes that it took us to get to Merrill Field, and I managed my second really okay landing of the trip.

So there we were, in Anchorage, pulling in to Take Flight Alaska (where I did my written exam some months ago…) and it was not quite 1 PM. Quinn's flight out of Anchorage was scheduled for 10 PM, so after all that fretting, we actually got him to Anchorage in time. What's more, it is a three hour flight to King Salmon in our little bugsmasher, and the last flight from King Salmon to Anchorage was scheduled to leave King Salmon at 6 PM (and arrives at 7:20… they fly a little faster than 624A…).

The brakes were getting a bit mushy again, so I asked for some help at Take Flight Alaska getting that dealt with, filled the tanks, then parked it for a few minutes while I went to get a briefing for the King Salmon leg.

But when I went in to the restroom, I emerged a few minutes later to see Quinn sitting in the Take Flight Alaska lounge chatting with another pilot. And sitting next to him were his bags. As in, he unloaded his stuff.

"What am I supposed to think this means?" I asked, pointing to the bags.

"What do you think it means? I think I'm done."

"We haven't even checked King Salmon weather yet!"

"Yeah… I made it here and I really don't want to push my luck at this point."

I guess he really did intend not to miss his flight. Of course his family is one very significant factor. Another is that his company works on a weekly schedule for leave, so if he wasn't there at the beginning of the work week it was likely pretty complicated. As in he might lose more than an extra day of time off. Which is understandable… I guess…

That left me without a plan for how to get home. I decided to check weather so I'd know how hard to plead with him and/or how hard to find another sucker… errr… I mean pilot… to help me get to King Salmon.

But the briefer didn't get very far, as Anchorage was barely flyable and the first weathercam beyond Anchorage on my route was showing solid IFR.

Sigh.

Deep breath.

We succeeded in meeting our primary objective for the day, which was Anchorage, and I definitely didn't have weather or pilot assistance to make any other moves, so I elected to call my friends in Anchorage and be happy to spend the night. And I started thinking about who might be able to help me.

I made a couple calls and found one gentleman who said he would talk to me the next day, but he wasn't sure. While I was sitting there in the Take Flight

PAMR. The bug-smasher behind bars, safely waiting at Merrill Field, at what turned out to be the end of Quinn's journey. I was left to round up another instructor for the remaining leg to King Salmon, because Quinn was out of time.

Alaska lounge on my cell phone, Quinn was chatting with the other pilot, whose name was Bryson, about our trip.

Bryson turned to me, "When are you going to take the plane on to King Salmon?"

I realized that Quinn had gone through his entire explanation without clarifying that I was a work in progress, unsafe at any speed, except perhaps sitting still on the ground. But maybe not even then.

"Actually, I'm only a student pilot. I've been in training throughout this trip. I have a lot of hours now, but I haven't even soloed yet. If you know of an adventurous pilot that might be interested in a scenic trip to King Salmon, I'm going to need some help getting the plane home."

He looked thoughtful, pulled out his cell phone, and dialed. Whoever he was calling didn't answer, so he left a message and put his phone away. A couple minutes later he confessed that he himself wasn't available the next day, because he had limited opportunity for hangar time and tomorrow was it for getting some work done on his own aircraft, which he was scheduled to assist with. But if I was thinking of leaving Monday... he would be willing to go along.

So we agreed to make contact the following day, and I left with Quinn to get some fast food, sit around my buddy Brian's house, and generally do nothing. All in all, a pretty good day. And Quinn did indeed make his flight.

But I had another flight to make... somehow...

DAY 13

In which I line up an instructor for the
flight home and prepare the airplane for a
cold weather departure the next day

As luck would have it, Sunday dawned absolutely beautiful. I attended a bible study with my friends, then my cell phone rang. The pilot I'd called initially the day before, the one that had said he'd think about it and call me was calling to say that he would be willing to go with me... on Monday.

I told him I had another option for Monday and while I'd be happy to have his help, I could get there without him at this point if it was an issue. He encouraged me to check and see whether Bryson was a CFI, in which case I should see whether he would be willing to let me fly so I could log the hours.

So I called Bryson and he was in fact still interested, he was in fact a CFI, and he was in fact willing to let me fly and give me feedback on where I was. What an opportunity! He used to teach at Take Flight Alaska, but now was flying commercially up out of Kotzebue, and was in Anchorage on days off. His CFI wasn't due to expire for a few months. I told him I was going to go and check on the plane and try to figure out a way to keep the wings covered and was looking to round up a heater.

As it turned out, when we got there the wings had a good layer of frost still on them at 3 PM. My friend Brian and I spent an hour or so working on the frost, with the plane repositioned to be in the full sunlight, until we got it truly cleaned off. We used the little brush on the windshield scraper in Brian's car. It did an admirable job, coupled with some good elbow grease. We took turns, but I think Brian did a better job than I did.

The sun had been shining all day, but it never topped 20F, and the frost was not leaving. We had brought a big long piece of plastic tarp that covered from one end of the wings to the other, and after cutting a strategic hole to allow us to slide it on around an antenna, we stretched it over the wings and fastened it with an only-in-Alaska combination of duct tape and twine. At least the following day we would not have frost on the wings.

While we were taking turns working on the frost problem, Brian and I were also taking turns watching airplanes. Merrill Field is a very busy airport, with multiple flight schools and many private airplanes. There are three runways, one of them unpaved. Unpaved runways are common in Alaska in some places just as a factor of cost; they are cheaper to build. But they also cause much less wear on tires.

For most tires, that would be a minor issue, and probably not worth the trade off of other damage. Propellers in motion tend to have a groundwash beneath them that picks up loose items, including gravel, and can lead to propeller damage or wear in addition to damage to other trailing surfaces such as gear and horizontal stabilizers. It is much cheaper to replace tires than to replace a propeller or do extensive work on a horizontal surface.

But tundra tires are different, especially the super oversized, super soft, and floppy Alaska Bushwheels. Bushwheels are huge, and they allow airplanes to land on terrain that is pretty uneven compared to regular tires. But the soft rubber gets worn off pretty quickly on pavement, and those tires, unlike my tires, are really expensive, so pilots like to avoid pavement with them when possible.

We were adjacent to runway 07-25, and traffic was on runway 07. I watched a few different aircraft doing touch and goes, and it was fascinating to watch. I watched a Cessna 152 repeatedly coming in and landing almost half the distance down the runway, wobbling and jerking all the way, and then leaping off again for the next try. The look of those landing attempts was familiar, I could almost feel the sense of overwhelming workload and frustration. At least, that's what I felt like when my landings looked more like that.

There were a few planes that were landing a little better than that, but then there was a Cessna 180 flying the pattern. That airplane was landing within 100 feet of the beginning of the runway. That's right, of the beginning of the runway.

He was back off the runway by the time he got anywhere near us, I'd estimate within 300 feet of where he touched down. And he did that over, and over, and over. Wow. I don't think I ever thought about the practice that goes into flying in tight situations.

A pilot I know in King Salmon told me that he likes to make every takeoff a practice for short-field, so he always looks down the runway and estimates where he will be off, then tries to beat that mark. The gentleman in the 180 at Merrill Field was practically putting on a short takeoff and landing (STOL) clinic. But he was practicing at Merrill Field, where he had all kinds of room. When he got somewhere else, where he didn't have so much room, he'd know exactly what he could do. It was awe-inspiring to watch.

Watching all those airplanes flying the pattern made me want to do the same. I hadn't had a chance to practice pattern work since we left Ohio, and I felt like I'd learned an awful lot in that time, such that the pattern flight that was so completely overwhelming before was an attractive challenge now. I was reasonably confident that I could land the airplane safely (and consistently) now, yet I had only done two pattern flights, and they were days ago. I realized later, in going over my log book, that after our arrival in Anchorage I had only logged 39 landings total. I was certainly not ready for a STOL contest, but I was very interested in practicing. But, that would have to be later.

Around the time we finished putting on our low-grade wing covers, Bryson arrived. He dug around and borrowed a cowling cover and a small space heater, then put the heater under one of our cowls and we battened down the cowling cover. We agreed to meet Monday around 10 AM or thereafter and talked a bit about survival gear and where I was in training. He was pleased to hear that I had a full stash of survival gear on board, but said he planned to bring his own as well.

And with that, we called it an afternoon and headed off to meet again the following day for the final leg of the Columbus to King Salmon odyssey.

DAY 14

In which I work on correcting my altitude issues,
make a landing in King Salmon, Alaska, and get
some independent feedback on my flying skills

Monday morning was just dawning when I arrived at Take Flight Alaska to prepare the plane for flight. The junk yard quality wing covers had worked fabulously, and were completely covered with frost while the wings themselves were happily frost-free beneath them. But the frost was pretty solid on the rest of the plane. The horizontal stabilizers and the fuselage behind the wings had lots of frost on them, so I spent a long time patiently removing frost. When my hands got cold, I'd watch other plane operators doing the same thing. Most of them seemed to use large push brooms on their wings to thoroughly rake the surfaces. I wasn't sure that was okay for fabric wings like I had, so I was using leather gloves to rub the frost off, which took a lot longer. But I had the frost removed before Bryson arrived, and had thoroughly preflighted the airplane when he showed up.

We again covered where I was in training: almost fifty flight hours but relatively few landings, flying with increasing comfort and confidence but with less experience in maneuvers and pattern than might be expected. We checked our survival equipment, went over the preflight list I had gone through, then made final preparations by removing covers and heater and getting in the plane for start-up. It started up easily, then as it sat to warm up we covered a few additional items.

Bryson felt comfortable having me fly the aircraft, but he elected to handle the radio in the busy and (for me) confusing Anchorage airspace. We discussed our departure options, which amounted to two target elevations. We could fly over downtown Anchorage and then cross Cook Inlet at either less than 600 feet or greater than 2,000 feet.

"Six hundred feet is just not much room over Cook Inlet…"

Actually, we both were very unimpressed with the 600 foot option, but there was very little time for climbing to 2,000 feet by the time we reached the inlet, especially in our little climb-challenged pony.

"Have you looked at the City High departure procedure?"

"No, what is that?"

"Here, in the back of the Alaska Supplement, it provides departure procedures for Anchorage including Merrill Field."

Bryson showed me the documentation on the procedure, which allowed us to fly away from Cook Inlet toward Providence Hospital to the southeast of the airport in order to climb for the altitude we needed. Then, we would turn back to fly over Merrill Field and then Cook Inlet to the northwest.

By this time, we were warmed up and ready to taxi for engine run up and takeoff. Run up was done adjacent to the end of runway 25, but there is a prohibition on doing an engine run up while perpendicular to the runway in that location. This is due to the large number of airplanes that would be getting sandblasted by the propwash, as there is a parking area immediately adjacent to the taxiway at that location. So we turned and faced in the direction of the runway for our run up, completed our run up checklist, then turned back to face the runway while we waited for clearance. The traffic pattern was pretty full, and other planes were waiting on the other side. But after a couple of planes touched down, the plane across was cleared and he headed out onto the runway and off. Moments later we were cleared to take off, so we rolled onto the runway and away we went.

Bryson told me that he liked to put in the first notch of flaps before the takeoff roll for the added margin of safety, so I was doing my first flaps takeoff. The takeoff didn't seem any different than normal, but on climbout the airplane was slower with the notch of flaps. I was at Vx (best angle of climb) speed instead of Vy (best rate of climb speed), which is at the top end of the flaps operating range. We made the traffic pattern turn south in preparation for the City High departure procedure, climbing as we went. I pulled the notch of flaps out when we achieved Vy, and we flew over Providence Hospital before turning around and heading north for the crossing of Cook Inlet. On previous flights, Bryson had been allowed to fly in the altitude range that was reserved for military traffic going in and out of Elmendorf Air Force Base. But when we contacted Anchorage Departure Control, we were told to climb and maintain 2,500 feet. It appeared they were going to be keeping that airspace below for military use.

Our little engine that could chugged its way up to 2,500 feet just barely in time, and we were headed across the inlet. My paranoid scan caught a rather large bogey headed our way. Actually, it was well below us, and it was a very large military transport, headed into Elmendorf. I guess they really did need that airspace. We were probably more than 1,000 feet above it, but I still found I had to consciously avoid the instinct to climb. My airplane really wants to move away from all other traffic. At least, it does when my hand is on the controls…

After crossing Cook Inlet, we headed a little bit inland then turned south to fly along the Cook Inlet coast until we reached Lake Clark Pass. We were out of the Class C airspace, and Bryson okayed me to climb to the level I was comfortable for cruise. So I headed up for 4,500 feet.

We hadn't got halfway to that altitude from our previous one when the radio squawked, "Two four alpha, maintain 2,500 feet."

Confused, I looked at Bryson and started losing altitude. He calmly looked out the window, then keyed his mike, "Anchorage departure, two four alpha, requesting 4,500 feet."

"Two four alpha, what is your destination?"

"Two four alpha is headed for Lake Clark Pass on our way to King Salmon."

"Two four alpha, 4,500 feet approved."

It really hadn't occurred to me that ATC would try to control traffic altitude outside the controlled airspace, but they work an area much larger than the little circle on the map around Anchorage, primarily to allow them to manage traffic on the approaches into Anchorage. And, as I learned later, we were crossing one of the main approach routes for the large planes.

Both Quinn and Bryson are so calm and relaxed about dealing with ATC that it was inspiring. I hope to attain such a calm handle on communications as well. Luckily, King Salmon is a towered airport so I'll get lots of practice with a relatively low-level of traffic before I head back into more congested airspace.

One of the things I had told Bryson was that while I was flying comfortably, I was having difficulty pegging my altitude still. In truth, it was likely just a matter of my subconscious. When I called and gave Quinn a rundown of the flight to King Salmon and asked him what he had though about my altitude issues, he laughed and said he wasn't worried about my altitude issues because I was fully capable of holding at my altitude plus 100 feet, and he figured it would come with practice when I was more comfortable with the plane and flying in general. How right he was.

Bryson said that it is a good practice to take something like altitude and just make it a very conscious part of the scan, and to remove the leeway that is offered even in the practical test standards. He recommended that I establish the width of the indicator needle as my reasonable error for altitude, and that if that needle wasn't touching on my target altitude that I correct.

So that's what we started out to do. We flew down Cook Inlet at 4,500 feet, plus or minus perhaps 15 feet, and it worked. I was so concerned about keeping that altitude, in part because I had given myself very little leeway, that I found myself looking at the altitude indicator with great attention during my scan. And I would keep my scan active in part so I could get back to the altitude indicator. Very instructive. All these days of flying higher than I was supposed to, and now all of a sudden I was holding altitude like a pro. We passed over Tyonek, as well as an assortment of cabins and a couple other little settlements, and soon found ourselves looking for the entrance to Lake Clark Pass.

Lake Clark pass is probably the most trafficked route in and out of southwest Alaska, at least for small planes. It lies in the shadow of Mount Redoubt, which was calm at the time but started erupting six months later, virtually sealing off small plane travel for days and weeks at a time. But on our flight, it was merely part of the scenery as we headed down Cook Inlet.

Lake Clark Pass is a glacial valley that bridges the divide between the Cook Inlet and Bristol Bay drainages. The recession of glaciers has resulted in a long, low route from one side to the other.

I've flown through Lake Clark Pass before. Actually, I should say I've ridden through Lake Clark Pass before. I have a decent memory for landscape, probably related to my love for it, and I saw a little knoll near the entrance to a valley that looked like what I remembered at the entrance of Lake Clark Pass. But the valley seemed too narrow.

"I'm not sure that this is right..."

"Okay, what are you looking at that makes you think that? Let's look at the map."

Looking around, I could soon see that it was, in fact, the right one, and Bryson's smile confirmed that he had already known it and was just checking out my navigating skills. He almost got to see me flub a map exercise, something that would have been more precious if he'd known how rare that is.

But the narrowness of Lake Clark Pass was really astonishing to me now, in my first time at the controls. The pass makes two right-angle turns above a rubble-strewn valley bottom. The rubble is bordered by vegetation that extends up the valley walls for hundreds of feet before giving way to sheer rock faces. The sheer rock was before us and on either side. I'm not small, but I felt small right then. Flying through Lake Clark Pass cannot fail to impress any human with powers of vision.

Bryson was interested in my experience and background with mountain flying, so we talked about that a bit. I was especially interested in staying on the downwind side of the valley so that I would be riding an updraft and any turn would be into a headwind, giving more room. He seemed less set on that, but was willing to let me fly that strategy, and in we went.

The wind was from the north, so I held with the southern wall off the left wing tip. In this fashion, we made the two right angle turns, passing along next to glaciers spilling out from both sides and terminating in the valley bottom or up on the walls. We passed over the lake near the summit, which marked our transition from the Cook Inlet drainage to the Bristol Bay watershed.

We were looking to cut down through a valley that comes out at the very upper end of Lake Clark. As the valley came into view, it had a layer of clouds packed into it at around 2,500 feet.

"Okay, what are you going to do now?"

It looked like we could fly underneath it, but I didn't want to give up altitude. We could easily have flown over it, but it would obscure the terrain below, which would be really unfortunate in an emergency situation. So I opted instead to take the longer route down the Tlikikila (say that five times fast…) River Valley that comes out partway down the lake.

"I don't want to give up altitude, and I don't intend to fly above clouds. I'm expecting that you wouldn't want to be placed in a situation where you had to make an emergency landing that included passing through clouds?"

"No, I wouldn't."

"And since we have a perfectly viable alternate route with great visibility and ceiling straight ahead, I intend to fly that drainage, which comes out at where Lake Clark joins Little Lake Clark."

Bryson seemed satisfied with this, and off we went. At about this time, Bryson noted that I was not hugging the side of the pass, as I had intended, and suggested that I get away from the center, as it leaves less room for turning around. Before I got back over to the side of the valley, he followed that up by asking what I knew about left-turning tendencies of the airplane.

I listed off the left turning tendencies, which were familiar from my ground school studies and especially from takeoff, when the airplane is at high power and high angle of attack.

Bryson nodded, acknowledging that I had a book knowledge. But the practical relation of that to mountain flight was a connection I had not made. He pointed out that hugging the left wall means that in an emergency or to turn around, I have to turn right, against the direction the airplane naturally wants to turn, but that by hugging the wall to my right, any turn I would need to make would be assisted by the aeronautical properties of the airplane. A potentially important distinction in a narrow pass!

So that was why he was less set on holding the updraft side of the valley, because when it counters the left-turn tendency side it is a trade-off of one advantage for another. It turns out that another consideration is that in canyon or mountain flying, holding the right wall is the standard traffic pattern. In point of fact, we had not found any updrafts or downdrafts in the pass, so the right side was a better option, both from the standpoint of standard traffic and from the improved turning performance. From that point on, we flew along the right side of the valley. The rock wall out the right window was stunning, I half wondered whether we might look up and see sheep above us on the rocks...but we didn't. A few minutes on, we emerged from the valley where the river drained into Lake Clark.

"Should we cross the lake and fly down the steeper southeast shore that will take us over Port Alsworth, or stay on this side, which means we are further from people but can avoid crossing the water?"

Bryson looked thoughtful, "I'd be in favor of keeping nearer inhabited areas where we can."

I looked around, and the rather large isthmus of land that spills out from the mouth of the Tlikikila (brave enough to try to say that yet?) River almost completely crossed the lake.

"Look at that, we can cross the lake right here without being over water at all."

"I can't see what you are pointing at."

I turned the aircraft so he could get a look at the sandbar crossing the lake, then we crossed it and flew along over Port Alsworth and on down the lake. The valley as we flew along started to broaden, and the slope from the mountains to Lake Clark softened. Soon, we could see the multiple terraces carved by the lake over time as it dropped down. Glacial lakes usually recede over time, as the outlet river cuts down through the mass of rubble that the glacier pushed up at the end of the lake. Thousands of years of lake recession were reflected below us in steps filled with small potholes and terraced vegetation.

We flew on, while I fully enjoyed this final, glorious flight home. Soon, we reached the end of Lake Clark, and passed over Six Mile Lake, then the village of Nondalton. Off to the right of Nondalton, we could see ancient lava flows descending off the hill. After passing Nondalton, we flew into the Nondalton Gap, and finally hit our first downdrafts of the flight.

After my rather stellar altitude-maintaining performance on the first phases of the flight, I found I could not keep altitude in the drafts we were encountering. Bryson advised me not to worry about altitude until the air stabilized, and a few minutes later we switched from downdrafts to updrafts anyway.

As we were dealing with the first drafty air of the flight, we were also crossing over the area of the Pebble project. In this small, nondescript region of rural Alaska, mining interests have been evaluating the feasibility of one of the largest mines on earth. A gold, copper, and molybdenum deposit lies at the headwaters of three drainages, each part of the largest salmon fishery on earth. The record of water contamination from mines such as the proposed one is not comforting to fishermen. The mine company insists that their proposal should not be judged based on the past performance of similar mines, because they'll do things differently this time.

Bryson has been working in Kotzebue, where a substantial portion of the local economy is mining. The furor over the Pebble development has generated interest in Kotzebue because locals there are concerned that actions to limit the potential impact of Pebble would hurt the ability of the Red Dog Mine out of Kotzebue. Which would hurt their economy.

As for me? Mining is a fact of modern life, and unless we stop buying things made of the mined materials, the feasibility of the mine is partially our own fault. But I do feel that the mine proposers should have to demonstrate that they have made every attempt to avoid toxic downstream (both in terms of surface water and groundwater) impacts. And I have to profess it does seem like past performance is exactly what the proposal should be judged on...

From the Pebble site, it was on to the end of Iliamna Lake, then across the Kvichak (it's not pronounced like it looks... try kwee-jack...) River and on a direct heading toward King Salmon. We passed over the Alagnak River and started to descend slightly at 20 miles out.

"This is a reporting point for inbound traffic, it's called Gooneybird Hill."

Bryson turned to look at me, "Gooneybird? That's the name of an airplane."

"Yeah, there's one parked on the hill in scattered fragments. Apparently they tried to scoot in under the weather and found the hill at high speed... You might be able to see some parts."

As we passed over the hill, we checked the automated weather, then called in and were advised to check back when we were one mile out.

Meanwhile, after a very good flight, I was trying to get myself ready for the landing. Wind was from 330 at 20, giving a crosswind component of 10 knots on runway 36. I descended to pattern altitude in time, which was good as I seemed to have finally reached the point where that was not as difficult to plan. Before we even keyed the mike to announce one mile out, the tower cleared us to land.

"Two four alpha, clear to land runway 36."

As we flew left downwind for 36, we were at pattern altitude and at pattern airspeed of 80 mph. So far, so good. We turned base, and brought in one notch of flaps. On base, Bryson turned to me, "When do you drop your approach speed down to around 70 mph?"

"When you get below 80 mph, the sink rate increases pretty quickly, so even though it stalls around 50, we tend to hold 80 almost all the way to the flare."

He looked thoughtful. Perhaps disbelieving... I'm not sure what he thought of that. But as we turned base, and I tried to get stabilized to bring in the second notch of flaps (which I was feeling ready to use, these days), the airspeed dipped below 80 and he murmured, "I see what you mean."

I wasn't feeling perfect about the final approach, but we were in a stabilized descent toward the aiming point and landed using a total of 1,700 feet of runway, then taxied over to the hangar.

There to greet us was Paul, as well as both our families. Paul opened up the hangar so we could get the airplane in and he could look it over. Which was sure to be a detailed inspection. Paul is an incredibly detail-oriented person, and his work products are flawless, so I knew it would be an education for both of us.

In the meantime, Bryson suggested that I could use some more practice on crosswind landings. Hard to disagree. I had now a total of 40 landings in my logbook. When I asked for more detail, he said I was a bit late getting stabilized and not as smooth as I should have been.

"Where do you feel I am at this point in training, after our flight today?"

"Well, after a flight in the pattern with you, I would be comfortable signing you off for solo."

!!!!!!!!

Wow!

I'd sort of stopped thinking about solo since Quinn and I had realized that there would be no way for me to finish during the trip. Before we left, I had been scared of solo flight anyway, just completely unprepared. Now, I hadn't been thinking about it, but it didn't scare me. So that's probably a good situation. In the meantime, I had attained the dubious status of being the highest time pre-solo student pilot that I had ever heard of.

We sent Bryson back to Anchorage that evening and I set about trying to equilibrate to life back at home and to assess where I was. Quinn and I hadn't spoken about my progress in some time, so I decided to ask him where he thought I was. But I didn't want him to know what Bryson thought, so I just sent him an email asking.

His response?

"Based on the last few landings you should be ready to solo."

He went on to point out that the regulations, "require training in a few areas prior to solo including ground reference maneuvers," which I had not done, so I would need to get an introduction to some of those.

"However, the most time consuming area to work on pre-solo is getting to the point where you are consistently making good approaches and landings. Your last few have been good and getting better so you should be right there."

So it appears that a few flights before leaving and a cross-country journey to Alaska firmly established me in the 'almost ready to solo' camp.

I was to be stuck in that camp for months, because Paul and I elected to pull the aircraft apart and start on the long first annual before additional flight. In the back of my mind, for the months when we were working on recreating the plane in nearly new fashion, was, "When can I do that again?"

16 MONTHS LATER

Yes, you read that right … 16 months …

The winter after I arrived in King Salmon with the airplane had been spent pulling it apart to the roots and putting it back together. We cleaned up and repainted a few parts, completely replaced others, cleaned out the entire thing, checked everything we could imagine, and then spent hours running the engine and checking instruments, oil pressure, everything you could check on the ground. We got a friend of ours to come and take it for a flight to verify that it was all in good shape. I lined up an instructor, Jim, and sent him off for a flight to get familiar with the airplane. Then, finally, after only seven months, I started flight training again. But there were a few things that didn't seem right, as we were having a lot of trouble starting the plane. So we grounded it and tried to figure out the issues, but summer had arrived. So the opportunity to get things dealt with was pretty sporadic during the busy season.

Much of the wiring in the aircraft appeared to be vintage 1950s installation. We had replaced quite a bit of it, but the process of working over the airplane appeared to have destroyed some of the integrity that those old wires had. So we replaced more, and soon had replaced most every wire there was to replace.

Finally, after ruling out a wiring problem, replacing the battery, and scratching our heads, we identified the starter itself as the problem. So we got a new starter and we were good to go. All of a sudden the airplane started enthusiastically. It turned out that the old starter had... a broken wire. Inside the starter. Why it ever worked was somewhat of a mystery...

So training started up in earnest 11 months after I arrived in King Salmon with the airplane. That much lag time necessarily resulted in a relearning curve, but I had still had a lot to learn anyway. But I worked my way through flying solo, to flying solo cross countries, night flight with Jim, and finally to the moment of truth. I was finished with all the experience, maneuvers, and training required to take my check ride. To see if I could actually become a private pilot.

Jim reviewed the areas of knowledge that constituted the areas I had missed on the knowledge test, and we looked for a flight examiner for my practical examination, or check ride. There are no examiners in King Salmon, so I was going to need to fly to the location of one of the examiners. The closest ones were in Bethel and Soldotna, and Jim was in favor of Soldotna, so we contacted the one in Soldotna and began to make arrangements.

Jim was hoping to fly in with me, but like all of us, he had responsibilities at home.

As did I.

The first good weather window after I was ready for the exam didn't come until we had been waiting for almost three weeks. Jim was just preparing to leave on a family vacation, so he and I discussed the conditions for the flight, he signed a solo endorsement for a cross country flight to Soldotna, and we parted at the airport. He got on a commercial flight to head to Disneyland, and I headed over to the other end of the airport to get N624A ready, went to work to attend a meeting I really needed to be present for, then called for a weather brief, filed a flight plan, and blasted off for Soldotna. In the air, I tried to open my flight plan.

"Kenai Radio, Tri-Pacer 624 alpha broadcasting on King Salmon VOR 122.2."

Silence.

I tried again... more silence. I couldn't get a response from Kenai Flight Services. Finally, I called back to King Salmon Tower.

"King Salmon Tower, Tri-Pacer 624 alpha."

"Tri-Pacer 624 alpha, King Salmon Tower."

"Yeah, 624 alpha is unable to raise Kenai Radio on the King Salmon VOR. Is there a maintenance issue?"

"Not that we're aware of, but we can open your flight plan for you, would you like us to do that?"

"That's an affirmative."

"Standby."

So I did. Well, I guess you could call it standing by, but really I was flying by, or in relation to the King Salmon Airport, I was flying away.

"Tri-Pacer 624 alpha, King Salmon Tower."

"This is Tri-Pacer 624 alpha, go ahead."

"Your flight plan is activated with Kenai Radio, and they report that the VOR transmitter is working, so the problem may be on your end."

"Okay, copy. Thank you."

Another strange thing. Why is everything always strange with flying? The radio works fine for King Salmon Tower, but not Kenai Radio? I didn't really believe that… it just didn't add up. So I kept on, heading north past the Alagnak River, then past Igiugig.

Then I encountered a troubling situation. I was monitoring 122.9, the common traffic frequency used in most of the Bristol Bay region. But Igiugig had recently switched to a CTAF of 122.8, so I was getting ready to switch frequencies to check in with traffic around Igiugig, when a transmission came over 122.9…

"Igiugig traffic, Bonanza WXYZ is five miles north, inbound for Igiugig." (Okay, I admit it, the call sign wasn't WXYZ, but I don't remember what it was…)

So… the CTAF had been recently changed, but here was a guy coming in and using the old one. It seems obvious now, I should have alerted him to the change. But I was only a student pilot. I had heard the same plane fly into Igiugig before on one of my solo cross countries before they changed the CTAF (…okay, actually I only think it was the same, as there aren't too many Bonanzas running around Bristol Bay, but I actually can't confirm that…). So I flew along, thinking that maybe the FAA had tried to change the CTAF but the locals didn't want to change. Perhaps that really is what happened. But it bugged me… so I asked my examiner about it after arriving. And he confirmed my feeling… I should have broadcast a notice that the CTAF had been changed. Next time…

Anyway, I flew on past Igiugig, around Lake Iliamna, and then along past the Iliamna Airport. I called Kenai Radio again… and got static in response.

"Kenai Radio, Tri-Pacer 624 alpha, you are broken, I do not copy."

The next transmission came through just fine.

"Tri-Pacer 624 alpha, Kenai Radio."

"Yeah, 624 alpha is giving a position update, I'm passing the Iliamna Airport."

"Okay, position updated, let us know if there is anything else we can do for you, if you need any weather updates, and please pass along any pilot reports."

"Okay, copy, thank you."

And thus started a strange sequence. Every time I called Kenai Radio, I couldn't understand them on their initial response, but then after telling them that, I could hear them clearly every time on the second try. In fact… the same problem followed me on the way back home. I am suspicious at this point that there is a bad transmit button on the equipment in the Kenai Flight Service Station.

I flew on past Nondalton, past Port Alsworth, and then started up Lake Clark Pass. It was a beautiful day, probably almost as beautiful as the day I had flown out from Anchorage 16 months before, and I hugged the south wall and looked at the Tlikikila (there's that word again…) River below. I realized that I was a very different pilot now, because I looked down and saw large expanses of sand bars that I realized made excellent emergency landing sites. Sixteen months before, nothing looked like a good emergency landing site.

I climbed as I went through the pass, because my calculations suggested I needed 4,500 feet of altitude to cross Cook Inlet at the Kenai Forelands, which is a point 9 nautical miles wide. Emerging from the pass, I broadcast my position and intentions on the West Cook Inlet CTAF of 122.7, then checked Kenai Airport weather and checked in with the Kenai Tower. They approved my request to descend through their airspace toward Soldotna, then approved a frequency change, and I went to the Soldotna CTAF of 122.5. I flew around to the south of the airport to enter midfield right downwind for runway 7, which has a right traffic pattern. In addition, the traffic pattern is low, at 900 feet msl, which is less than 800 feet agl. I found as I approached the airport that the downwind leg is only a few hundred feet above a ridge that runs parallel to the airport.

I came in and landed, then immediately took off and flew another pattern just to get another look at the nonstandard traffic pattern, landed again, and taxied off. Then I taxied around like a fool, looking for someplace that I could tie down. There had been a bunch of rain on snow, and the entire airport was covered in ice. I finally realized that I would have to dig through ice to get to the tie downs, identified the transient parking, and went there to excavate a way to secure the airplane.

So there I was. I had flown to Soldotna with a one-way endorsement for a cross country. The next day I would have a flight exam. If I passed, I'd get to fly home at my discretion. If I failed, I'd be stuck. I'd have to get remedial training to address deficiencies before I could retake the exam, and would be unable to fly away from Soldotna without finding an instructor to help.

The pressure was on…

THE CHECK RIDE

Or, how to combine more stress, disappointment,
and elation into one day than is healthy or wise

I'm not sure I can even keep it all straight in my own mind, to be honest. The designated pilot examiner asked a lot of questions about everything, including passenger maladies of various sorts, chart information, looking over my flight plan for the flight he asked me for, went over the airworthiness papers for the airplane in detail, as well as my own logbook and paperwork. I'm not sure there was much left out. The oral started at 12 noon, and really didn't end until we got in the airplane to fly, which was sometime around 3:30 or 4:00 PM. The flight started out fine, we took off with a soft-field takeoff and headed out from PASX toward Skilak Lake, then turned north following our flight plan to PAMR. Then, all of a sudden, it turned out that we heard of really bad weather ahead, but there appeared to be some good weather over 5K5, so I turned toward the southwest, pulled out the map, then tried to establish a heading. I did that by verifying the location of the bay in the distance, but checked it against the map. Then, we inexplicably flew into a cloud, and I couldn't see anything but the instrument panel. My passenger thought he might know where to find some better weather, so he offered a couple headings, which I turned to, but that didn't work. Then he thought that maybe if we could just find a way to get to PAEN it would help us out, so I dialed in the VOR and headed that way. At that point, the passenger took over the controls, and I was temporarily incapacitated. The passenger didn't really seem to know what he was doing though, as when he returned the controls to me the plan was in a left descending turn at about 120 mph, so I had to recover from that. Unfortunately, I was soon incapacitated again, and the passenger had us in a climbing right turn on the verge of a stall when I again came to and got us out of that situation. But then, suddenly, we broke out of the clouds and everything was better. I flew a couple steep turns, and had an altitude variation that was uncomfortably close to the 100 feet limit, but noticed and corrected in the turn, coming out within 20 feet of the initial altitude. The opposite direction steep turn was better, very steady all the way around. Then we did some slow flight. I dialed it back to 65, with flaps, and found myself far enough behind the power curve that I couldn't keep altitude, so before I busted altitude I sped up, dropped the flaps, climbed back up and started over. Then, when we were established in a firm mush, I plowed a couple shallow turns to headings. After that, we tried a power-off stall, then a power-on stall, then we did both stalls while turning. To this point, I felt okay, it had gone fairly well, I thought.

Then my passenger wanted to see a turn around a point, and he wanted to see it at 600 feet agl, so I identified a point, descended and got set up, and flew a beautiful egg-shaped pattern around a point. He really thought that wasn't quite what he had in mind, so he asked me to try again, at which I flew a cross between an egg and a circle, which he muttered about, but said it was time to return to the airport at PASX for takeoffs and landings. On the way there, at what I suspect was around 1000 agl, my engine failed. I quickly ran through the checklist, glide speed, place to land, carb heat, fuel, (oops, missed mixture...which he pointed out) and noticed that the place I wanted to land was going by under us too quickly. I failed to recognize that in time to choose a better place, and in focusing on the initial place overshot my glide speed, and, well, luckily the engine started up again, because we were headed for the trees. At that point, I thought I had just failed the engine out. It was surely the worst engine out I've flown recently. Nevertheless, he didn't say anything other than that I had made a mistake on my checklist, missing the mixture, and had given up a bunch of altitude when I got too fast. Then, inexplicably, my airspeed indicator failed. He looked at the black instrument cover and commented that it looked like the airspeed indicator had failed. I had to agree, and wondered whether it might in fact start working again before we got to the airport. He didn't think it would. As it turns out, he was right. So I flew along, trying to figure out how to fly without my crutch, I mean airspeed indicator, and I flew a normal landing, which turned out okay, though I was totally rattled. So there I am, on the tarmac, and he wants a short-field takeoff. Then, he decides at the last minute, while I'm going through my pre-takeoff checklist, to give back the airspeed indicator. I was already flustered and forgot to take off flaps. So we start our takeoff roll, go airborne, and then are mushing in the air at 60mph when I realize that I've got flaps in and we are failing to climb at all. I brought the nose down and popped out a notch of flaps, but instead of dropping one notch I dropped both, at which point we bounced, yes that's right, we bounced, then flew off into the pattern. Then I knew I had failed. He noted that I had missed an item on my pre-takeoff checklist, the flaps. I sure had. Next we came around for a short-field landing and normal takeoff, then a soft-field landing. But as we approached the runway at about 30 agl he saw something on the field, so I initiated a go-around. He said we missed whatever it was on the runway, so that was good. Then we did a soft-field landing and kept on rolling and he said it was time to taxi off. At that point I figured I was going to need retrained on a couple maneuvers. But when we debriefed he went through the entire test, beginning to end, and mentioned everything that I had done. Apparently the fact that I had addressed my issues and responded to the problem safely, even with the bounce, was what he was needing to see in those situations. So the retraining will happen, but it won't be required for me to get my certificate...because I already have it. The temporary one anyway. The last couple patterns he helped me make a couple of changes to the way I was flying them, but now I have to relearn everything.

I stopped in PAIL and had a hilarious landing where I was going way too fast and floated halfway down the runway. Then when I left, I thought a gravel access road, which I had floated past on landing, was a taxiway, so I soldiered off to that end of the apron and went cross country to the runway. Folks must have had a chuckle watching me leave. Oh well, I'm more familiar with PAIL now.

So that's my story. I slept the sleep of the dead Tuesday night, but I kept waking up seeing short-field takeoffs that involve a bounce. The flight home yesterday helped cure that though, so I'm feeling pretty okay. But I need lots of practice. Today took my mechanic partner for his first ride in our plane, which was very rewarding, so that was a bonus as well.

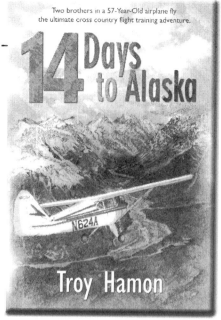

Two brothers in a 57-Year-Old airplane fly
the ultimate cross country flight training adventure.

14 Days to Alaska

Troy Hamon

To contact Troy Hamon for book signings or to arrange for him
to be a guest speaker for your group, call or email:
Phone: (907) 469-0343 ••• trhamon@yahoo.com

USE THIS COUPON TO ORDER ADDITIONAL COPIES

Please ship to:

First Name _____ Last Name _____

Address _____

City _____ State _____ Zip _____

Phone Number _____ email _____

		Quantity	Total
Orders shipped via Air Mail the day they are received.	14 Days $17.95 each	_____	$ _____
	Shipping and Handling 3.00 each		$ _____
	No S and H with purchase of two books or more. **Grand Total**		$ _____

Credit Card Number _____ ❏ VISA

Expiration Date _____ Signature _____ ❏ MC

Publication Consultants

MasterCard 8370 Eleusis Drive, Anchorage, Alaska 99502 VISA
phone: (907) 349-2424 • fax: (907) 349-2426
www.publicationconsultants.com — email: books@publicationconsultants.com

Made in the USA
Middletown, DE
29 October 2017